LAWS THAT CHANGED AMERICA

Jules Archer
History for Young Readers

LAWS THAT CHANGED AMERICA

JULES ARCHER

Foreword by Brianna DuMont

Sky Pony Press

NEW YORK

Historical texts often reflect the time period in which they were written, and new information is constantly being discovered. This book was originally published in 1967, and much has changed since then. While every effort has been made to bring this book up to date, it is important to consult multiple sources when doing research.

Sky Pony Press books may be purchased in bulk at special discounts for sales promotion, corporate gifts, fund-raising, or educational purposes. Special editions can also be created to specifications. For details, contact the Special Sales Department, Sky Pony Press, 307 West 36th Street, 11th Floor, New York, NY 10018 or info@skyhorsepublishing.com.

Sky Pony® is a registered trademark of Skyhorse Publishing, Inc.®, a Delaware corporation.

Visit our website at www.skyponypress.com.

10 9 8 7 6 5 4 3 2 1

Library of Congress Cataloging-in-Publication Data is available on file.

Print ISBN: 978-1-63450-176-7
E-book ISBN: 978-1-5107-0709-2

Series design by Brian Peterson
Cover photo credit Thinkstock

Printed in the United States of America

TO THREE ESTEEMED PEOPLE,
IN APPRECIATION:

Congressman Joseph Y. Resnick
Lawyer Robert Zicklin
Agent Edith Margolis Keyshore

The author gratefully acknowledges the help of Daniel S. Holier, Administrative Assistant to Congressman Joseph Y. Resnick of the 28th District, New York, and of the author's wife, Eleanor, in the extensive research that went into the writing of this book.

Jules Archer
Pine Plains
New York

CONTENTS

6. LAWS THAT DEVELOPED OUR RESOURCES   48

Flood That Threatened the War Effort

7. LAWS FOR THE WORKER   56

Massacre in South Chicago

13. LAWS FOR SOLDIERS AND SCHOLARS 110

Draft Riots In New York

FOREWORD

Laws seem like a whole lot of "don'ts". Don't speed. Don't walk around naked. Don't litter. Don't kill anybody. It's true that laws rule our daily life, but they also span the spectrum from our daily don'ts to our yearly do's—like paying taxes. Whether we think about them or not, laws are constantly there, running our country, ruling our behavior, and creating our society. Almost everything we do is molded by laws.

It wasn't always that way in America. The Founding Fathers had an every-man-for-himself mindset. They didn't want citizens to lose that DIY quality, and they were convinced that security nets like welfare for the poor or even equal education laws would make the country weak and reliant on others. They didn't realize they could also make us strong. Now, laws protect our money, our health, and our environment, just to name a few.

With so many laws, perhaps it's not surprising to learn that experts estimate that regular John and Jane Doe break about seven laws a day, often without even knowing it. That includes you! Did you know, singing copyrighted songs in a public setting is infringement? Or crossing a street anywhere except at a crosswalk with the little person lit up is jaywalking? Well, it is.

Even the federal government doesn't know how many laws there are! They tried to count them all in 1982 and eventually gave up. Hopefully you don't get busted for breaking some archaic law, like playing bingo for five hours and one minute in North Carolina. Or eating hamburgers on a Sunday in St.

Cloud, Minnesota. (Definitely don't barter your pet's fur for candy in Connecticut.) Luckily for you, Jules Archer has done a lot of the heavy lifting. In this book, he lays out the most important laws that have shaped America. Break these and you'd definitely be in trouble.

The first set of laws Archer covers "open up" the continent. Here, he introduces America's stories of settlement and, sadly, slavery in these new, open territories. The early days of American history weren't always what you might consider "civilized", but they still had their legal systems and laws governing people's lives. It took almost a hundred years, but eventually there were laws that outlawed slavery, too.

Next, Archer runs through banking laws, which helped protect our money and stabilize our economy. These are of particular interest to us today, as experts debate whether the partial repeal of the 1933 Glass-Steagall Act by President Bill Clinton in the 90s led to the 2007 Recession.

Pay close attention to the third chapter, which delves into the most basic American rights—the Bill of Rights. You don't have to worry about secret police knocking down your door in the middle of the night, ripping through all your belongings, and quickly hauling you off to jail for some undisclosed reason. That's how important the Amendments are. They protect the rights of the accused, free speech, free assembly, and freedom of religion.

As Archer points out in chapter four, some subsequent laws are pretty scary. He blames war hysteria for the "red-white-and-blue" laws that subverted our freedoms. If Archer were writing this today, he'd probably add the Patriot Act of 2001 into that batch, which allows the government to investigate anything they believe is related to terrorism. That can include your telephone records, your house, and even your record of checked-out library books if they sound suspicious.

The next few chapters jump into laws that shaped foreign policy, workers' rights, and business rights. You'll see some that protect us, like the laws in chapter nine on health, education, and welfare. If it wasn't for them, you could be up at two a.m. canning broccoli for two cents a day instead of learning at school. (Yes, this sort of child labor happened.)

Some examples in this book might feel outdated, like the chapter on farmers' rights. The 30s, 40s, and 50s seem like ancient history to us. The Internet wasn't even a twinkle in Al Gore's eye. (Note: Despite what the Internet tells you, Al Gore did not invent it.) But Archer lived and wrote during a time when things like the Great Depression, Senator Joseph McCarthy's Red Scare, and Civil Rights were current, or at least recent, events. For us, they're equally important to discuss. Knowing the mistakes made in our past helps us understand how to grow and change, although some stories he recounts sound eerily similar to our own current events, including a race riot in LA in 1965. Sometimes we don't learn our history well enough.

Perhaps the biggest takeaway from Archer's book isn't about remembering our past. It's about appreciating how important the process is. Archer notes that what once seemed radical is now normal—like women voting and holding office. Women at the polls was shocking only a hundred years ago! That's the great thing about democracy—your voice counts. Some laws are here today, gone tomorrow. It isn't some dictator telling us exactly how to live our lives and issuing as many "don'ts" as he can invent. It's a give and take process between voters and lawmakers. Sure, it can seem long and tedious as a bill travels the winding road through Capitol Hill to the president's desk, but it's certainly better than waking up in a labor camp for the next twenty years on some ridiculous, trumped-up charge.

So the next time you go to school or buckle your seat belt, don't grumble. Think about the law you're obeying and how it serves you. And if it doesn't, remember, there are ways to change them. Study up and get involved in your government!

—Brianna DuMont

I

Laws that Opened Up America

"We Southerners object to the Homestead Bill," cried Representative Laurence M. Keitt, "because it is a fraud! It is a scheme by Northern speculators to grab public lands for private profit. Finally, we charge that Congress has no power to give land away to individuals."

When the peppery congressman sat down, the Speaker recognized Representative Galusha Aaron Grow, a six-foot-two, two-hundred-pound giant from Pennsylvania. He was a lawyer whose callused hands testified to his familiarity with an ax.

"If Congressman Keitt wanted to tell you the truth," he told the House coolly, "he would tell you the South objects to the Homestead Bill because it would open up the West to farmers, not plantation owners. He's afraid more free states will end Southern control of Congress!"

"Are you calling me a *liar,* sir?" yelled Keitt.

"Take it any way you want."

The enraged Southerner bounded across the aisle, swinging his cane at Grow's head. The huge Northerner grabbed the cane. Breaking it in two with his bare hands, he lashed out powerfully with his right fist. The blow staggered Keitt. Mouth bloody, he threw himself on the Pennsylvania congressman. The two men battered each other savagely.

A blow landed hard under Keitt's jaw and he went flying backward at an angle. As he crashed against another representative's desk, horrified solons rushed to stop the undignified brawl that had broken out in their midst.

"Order! Order!" roared the Speaker, banging his gavel. He was outraged that such an unruly scene could occur in Congress at so civilized a time as June, 1860.

The results were just as hectic. The Homestead Bill was passed by both houses of Congress. But President Buchanan vetoed it. Congressman Crow's bill—for he was the one who had introduced it—had to wait for a new climate, the next year's war Congress under President Lincoln, before he could see his dream of an expanded America become law.

The struggle to open up America to settlement and growth won its first great impetus in 1787, only four years after the Founding Fathers won their freedom from Britain, with the passage of the Northwest Ordinance. They knew that beyond the first Eastern mountain ranges there lay a tremendous unpopulated land waiting for ax and plow. The vexing question was: Who was to be given the right to settle and own it?

The soldiers who had fought in the Revolution understandably felt that they had a right to claim homesteads in the "wild lands" west of the seaboard. The American myth has been that all a pioneer had to do was to migrate westward, stake out a homestead, clear it, and it was his for the taking.

The real facts were a different matter. "It usually turned out," reports Stewart H. Holbrook in *Dreamers of the American Dream,* "that land sharks in one shape or another had got there ahead of him . . . in the form of a grantee-lord of whom he had never heard, or of a corporation he did not know existed."

Thus, if he had settled on, cleared, and developed a home-site, he was often dismayed to find that legal title belonged to someone else. And he was ordered to leave or be thrown off the property.

From the earliest times in America the value of land was fully recognized and exploited by businessmen who became widely detested as land sharks and land jobbers. They were so rich and powerful that they were even able to delay ratification of the Articles of Confederation. Maryland jobbers compelled other states to renounce claims to Western lands in favor of the central government—which the South hoped to dominate—before consenting to be part of the new United States.

The new government was so strapped for money that Congress almost immediately began to sell huge tracts of the wild lands at bargain prices. In 1787, a group of land speculators led by Manasseh Cutler, who wished to establish colonies in the Ohio country, induced the Continental Congress to adopt the Northwest Ordinance. Cutler, together with another land jobber, had obtained title to six million acres of wild lands. They wanted a government guarantee of law and order that would attract settlers to buy sites from them.

Congress obliged by establishing their lands as a Northwest Territory in 1787. The area, bounded on the south by the Ohio River and on the west by the Mississippi, later became the states of Ohio, Indiana, Michigan, Illinois, and Wisconsin.

Despite its profit-grubbing origin, the Northwest Ordinance proved to be the most important law passed by Congress under the Articles of Confederation. It set the pattern for future westward expansion of the United States.

The ordinance provided for local self-government when the male population reached 5,000, and for admission as a state when there was a population of 60,000. Settlers were guaranteed the rights of free speech, free press, religious freedom, trial by jury, and all civil liberties. Slavery was forbidden, education encouraged, and careful respect for the rights of Indians in the territory made mandatory.

Reassured that the Northwest Territory would be a safe and desirable place to homestead, pioneers from New York, New England, and Pennsylvania headed for the Ohio valley, joined by a stream of immigrant farmers fresh from Europe. Most had to buy their farms from the land jobbers, but they felt confident that the new wild lands would prove to be worth what they had paid.

Understandably, the Shawnee Indians of the region bitterly resented this invasion of their ancient homeland, and fought the settlers savagely for seven years. Then they were defeated and scattered in 1794 by an American expedition under General "Mad Anthony" Wayne. With the near West secured, the United States populated the Northern Territory to the bursting point until it was ready for the next big break-out.

Pressure for a new land law came when the frontier moved to the western side of the Mississippi. The new Republican Party responded to the hunger of farmers for cheap land in the West with the cry, "Vote yourself a farm!" But the Democratic South, loath to see antislavery spread westward, blocked land grants of the public domain to Eastern farmers.

Two years after the fist fight between Grow and Keitt on the House floor, America was plunged in civil war, and the Southern members had withdrawn from Congress. In May, 1862, the Republican Congress passed a new Homestead Act. It offered 160 acres of public land to anyone who agreed to cultivate it for five years and build his home there.

This historic act set off a westward migration that settled over 15,000 homesteaders on 2,500,000 cleared acres by the end of the Civil War. Soon after the early "nesters" moved into the vast areas of the plains and prairies, they were followed by hundreds of thousands of immigrants seeking a new life in Nebraska, Kansas, Iowa, Wisconsin, Minnesota, and the Dakotas.

The bill was not an unmixed blessing. Settlers quickly found that a 160-acre property was less than half the land needed in the semi-arid Great Plains for a bare living. Congress had to pass subsequent land measures increasing the holdings of landowners.

The bill was also full of loopholes that allowed the railroads, corporations, and speculators to grab millions of acres, many of which were resold to poor pioneers at a profit.

But despite its faults, the Homestead Act initiated the development of the West by transplanting several hundred thousand farmers onto its soil. More than a hundred million acres were under cultivation by the turn of the century.

In the same year that Congress passed the Homestead Act, it passed another bill of equal importance in opening up the West—the Pacific Railroad Act.

For years such an act had been stymied by the fight between North and South as to which cities ought to be linked by a national railroad. The South wanted a line that would run from Memphis through New Orleans and Texas to southern California. The North wanted a line that would let Eastern merchants ship goods from Chicago or St. Louis to the Northwest.

With the Civil War creating a Southern vacuum in Congress, no time was lost in granting a national charter to the Union Pacific Railroad to build a railroad from Nebraska to the northeast California border; and to the Central Pacific for another line meeting it from California. Congress gave the two lines 24,000,000 acres of public domain land, and loans totaling some $65,000,000.

"Can't we have a Pacific Railroad bill that don't stink of land-jobbing?" complained Horace Greeley, the famous *Tribune* editor whose advice, "Go West, young man!" had inspired hundreds of thousands of pioneers. "I hate to support one that smells of corruption!" But he did support it, recognizing its importance in opening the West.

Greeley's warning was accurate. The stockholders of the Union Pacific Railroad formed a construction company called the Credit Mobilier, whose profiteering plundered the federal treasury. Schuyler Colfax, vice-president under Grant, was exposed as part of the scandal, and was quickly dropped when the Grant administration sought a second term in office.

But the road was built, in an exciting race between the crews of East and West competing to see which could lay the most track. The Western laborers were largely Chinese, those of the East principally Irish immigrants. The two companies met at Promontory Point, Utah, on May 1, 1869.

As a golden spike was driven into the roadbed, marking the completion of America's first coast-to-coast railroad, cannon thundered in the nation's cities, firebells rang, and citizens paraded proudly.

"Think how the railroad has been pushed through this unwatered wilderness and haunt of savage tribes," wrote Robert Louis Stevenson, "how at each stage of the construction, roaring, impromptu cities, full of gold and lust and death, sprang up and then died away again; how in these uncouth places pigtailed Chinese pirates worked side by side with border ruffians and broken men from Europe, talking together in mixed dialect, mostly oaths, gambling, drinking, quarreling, and murdering like wolves. . . !"

But if the building of the Union Pacific was dramatic, its consequences for America were even more so. With swift, safe transportation guaranteed across the dangerous Indian lands and the treacherous Rockies, passengers and commerce flowed westward in hundreds, then thousands, then millions.

Within three years foreign trade with the Orient doubled. A tremendous cattle industry sprang up on the Great Plains. New towns and cities dotted the West in ever-increasing numbers. Soon new Western states were clamoring for admission to the Union. The last to be admitted in the continental United States was the 48th, Arizona, on February 14, 1912.

For almost half a century the forty-eight stars on the American flag seemed like a fixed, unchangeable number to Americans as well as to the rest of the world. They reflected the thinking of the nation that whatever outlying regions of the world might come under our administration in one form or another, the forty-eight states of the United States were now a closed club.

But for a long time there was constant pressure upon Congress by the people of its two major incorporated territories—Alaska and Hawaii—to admit them to statehood with the same rights and obligations as other states. America had purchased Alaska from Russia in 1867, and had taken Hawaii by force in 1893 after overthrowing its monarchy ruled by Queen Liliuokalani.

Congressmen who objected to statehood for Alaska pointed out that it was thinly populated and presented problems by not having a common border with any other American state. Those who objected to Hawaiian statehood referred to its 75 percent Pacific or Asiatic population, and the fact that it was 2,400 miles by air from continental United States.

Congressmen who demanded statehood for Alaska said that it was an extension of the principles laid down in the Northwest Ordinance of 1787, and that Alaska's strategic military location warranted it. Those who claimed statehood for Hawaii made the same arguments, and added that Hawaiians deserved it because of their loyalty to the United States during World War II.

It was the cold war, basically, that decided Congress to add two more stars to the American flag. The decision to admit

Alaska to statehood was in actuality a thinly disguised warning to the Soviet Union that any attack on Alaskan soil would be regarded as if it were an attack on Kansas or Connecticut.

There were three key policy reasons for the decision to admit Hawaii. First, if Alaska alone were admitted, all of the Orient would have good reason to conclude that Hawaii had been discriminated against by the United States for being nonwhite. Second, by admitting Hawaii, Congress hoped to persuade the people of neutral Asian nations to choose democracy rather than communism as their road to the future.

The third reason was to symbolize America's emergence as the leading world power, breaking out from her geographical isolation on the American continent by planting one of her states right in the middle of the Pacific Ocean. It was a not too subtle reminder to Red China that the United States considered the Pacific its legitimate back yard.

So on January 3, 1959, President Dwight D. Eisenhower signed the Alaska Statehood Act, and on March 18th of that same year, the Hawaii Statehood Act.

The flagmakers of America enjoyed a business boom selling the new fifty-star-spangled banners that marked the expansion of America's borders from the frozen tundras of the North to the swaying palms of tropical Honolulu.

2

Laws that Made us Prosperous

"There's a run on the bank! The Bank of the United States! Quick—get your money out before it's too late!"

"My God! Everything we own is in that bank!"

". . . but how can a bank owned by the government fail?"

"Hurry, *hurry!* Everything we've slaved for is in that bank—twenty-two years of hard work. Never mind dinner!"

Panic swept through the city of New York on December 11, 1931. Almost a half million New Yorkers had entrusted their savings to the Bank of the United States, which had no less than sixty branches throughout the city. Most of the depositors were working-class people who had believed that the bank, because of its name, was an instrument of the government.

It was not. The name was misleading, deliberately. It was a private bank, just as liable to failure as the 1,300 other banks throughout the country that had already shut their doors as a result of the crippling depression following the stock market crash of October 29, 1929. These bank failures had been kept as quiet as possible so as not to alarm the millions of Americans whose savings were in banks.

The rumors about the Bank of the United States spread over New York City like wildfire. Thousands, tens of thousands, then hundreds of thousands stormed the bank's branches, fighting for a place on line to withdraw their lifetime savings. People fainted, fights broke out, police had to be called to restore order. The bank tellers worked as slowly as possible, trying to stop the tremendous flow of money from being drained out of the bank's vaults.

It was obvious that the bank did not have the reserves on hand to meet these demands. Most of the assets were tied up in real estate investments that would take years to liquidate. The bank's executives could not borrow money from any other sources to pay off enough depositors to calm the panic and stop the run on the bank. They did the only thing they could.

They closed their doors and went into bankruptcy.

Hundreds of thousands of anguished New Yorkers, confident that they had been protected against the depression by a savings nest egg accumulated painfully over twenty or thirty years of hard work, suddenly found themselves penniless overnight. They were bewildered and outraged. Didn't the Bank of the United States *have* to pay them back their money? If it *wasn't* a government agency, why had it been allowed to use that name?

The whole American banking system, no longer commanding public confidence, teetered on the edge of collapse. One out of every four banks went under as people withdrew their money and hoarded it in stockings, jam pots, mattresses. With sources of credit cut off, many businesses had to close down, too.

Drastic action had to be taken to restore the confidence of the people in America's banks. On March 4, 1933, only two days after taking office as the new President, Franklin D. Roosevelt issued a special proclamation declaring a "bank holiday." All banks were temporarily closed to let the new Congress rush through emergency bank legislation giving the President control over all banking transactions.

On March 12th he broadcast his first "fireside chat" to the American people and reassured them, "It is safer to keep your money in a reopened bank than under the mattress."

But it took the Glass-Steagall Banking Reform Act, passed by Congress on June 16th, to restore the confidence of the American people in its nation's banks. This bill established the Federal Deposit Insurance Corporation (FDIC), a government agency, which guaranteed the savings of depositors.

If you look at your savings bankbook, you will see the little circle with the big word *insured* that is the result of the 1933 law. It protects each savings account up to the amount of $15,000. Thanks to this all-important law, it is safe for us to entrust our savings to banks.

Everyone benefits. We get interest on our savings. Businesses get the credit they need to prosper and create more jobs. People can borrow to build the homes they need. And you can be absolutely sure that any time you want to withdraw your money from the bank, you will get back every cent.

The first important law that helped make us a prosperous nation was passed in 1791. The country was in a precarious state financially at the end of the Revolutionary War in 1783. Many of the states had unpaid debts totaling $18 million. The national government owed another $56 million. Many men wanted to repudiate these debts, which would have destroyed the credit of the new republic. A government which has no financial support cannot survive, except as a military tyranny.

Alexander Hamilton, Washington's Secretary of the Treasury, devised a plan to win the financial support of the powerful men who controlled the Federalist Party—merchants, bankers, and speculators. He had the government assume the states' debts, and announced that *all* official debts would be honored in full. To establish a sound currency, he proposed a bill to establish a Bank of the United States that would be authorized to issue paper money, backed by gold, silver, and government bonds. Four-fifths of the bank's stock would be available to the Americans he esteemed—the "rich and well-born"—to provide an investment at a fat profit.

Thomas Jefferson, Washington's Secretary of State, was outraged at a plan he felt favored the rich creditor class over the poor debtor classes. Washington himself was in doubt about the constitutionality of the Federal Bank bill. He asked both Hamilton and Jefferson for opinions.

Fearful of extending the powers of an administration deeply committed to Federalist ideas, Jefferson wrote, "The incorporation of a bank, and the powers assumed by this bill, have not, in my opinion, been delegated to the United States by the Constitution." Hamilton argued that the Constitution gave "implied powers" to the government, which had the right to stretch clauses in order to get its work done.

Congress passed the bill and Washington signed it. The first Federal Bank did stabilize the government, at home and abroad, giving it the broad new powers it needed to survive and grow. Farmers, artisans, mechanics, and small shopkeepers—the debtor class—were angered by government favoritism toward the wealthy Federalists. They united behind Jefferson in a Democratic-Republican opposition to Hamilton.

The clash over the Federal Bank bill had far-reaching effects for future generations. Hamilton's "implied powers" theory of the Constitution gave future Presidents their argument for demanding laws which the Constitution did not specifically give the government the power to pass.

Another financial law of profound importance to every American was the Sixteenth Amendment proposed by Congress in 1909 and ratified on February 25, 1913, permitting the government to levy an income tax on all citizens. And ever since it has been the leading source of revenue for the nation's needs. Advocates of the income tax argue that it is the fairest form of taxation, based on the ability to pay. But no form of taxation has ever been popular, and the income tax is no exception.

President Woodrow Wilson, under whose administration the income tax became operative, admitted that truth when he wrote to Senator Oscar W. Underwood on the new law:

"Would it not be wise and fair," he urged, "to exempt all persons receiving less than $3,000 a year income from the necessity of making income returns at all, in order to burden as small a number of persons with the obligations involved in the administration of what will at best be an unpopular law?"

In 1961 the Commissioner of Internal Revenue, Dana Latham, himself acknowledged, "I think it is fair to say that the I.R.S. touches more directly and more intimately the lives of more American citizens than any other agency in Government . . . the Service is not a popular agency."

There has been fierce opposition to a federal income tax. During the Eisenhower administration, for example, the governor of Utah, J. Braken Lee, refused to pay his income tax to the Internal Revenue Service. Instead he placed the amount due in a local bank account. I.R.S. agents seized this account and placed a lien on all his bank accounts and private property.

There were earlier attempts at income taxes in American history. The first federal income tax was proposed to finance the war of 1812, but it was defeated, Lincoln saw to it that a federal income tax was passed to finance the Civil War, but it was terminated in 1872.

In 1894 President Cleveland succeeded in getting another income tax passed, but one year later the Supreme Court declared it unconstitutional. This was why the new law of 1909 had had to be passed in the form of a constitutional amendment.

The present I.R.S. has sought to make income taxes easier to pay, and tax forms less bewildering for the average man to fill out, by use of a "withholding tax." Under this system employers deduct estimated taxes owed from each weekly pay check, and forward them to the Revenue Service. At the end of the year it is only necessary for the taxpayer to fill out a "short form," adjusting whatever he still owes, or claiming an overpayment.

For many Americans, however, who have to claim special business deductions from their income, filling out income tax forms is a dreaded annual experience.

"The income-tax law is so complex," wrote Bernard M. Ward in his book *Man to Man,* "that neither the taxpayer, his counsel, the officials of the Bureau of Internal Revenue, nor the judges of the nation's courts understand it."

When Wilson came to office in 1913, a few tycoons in Wall Street wielded absolute control over the nation's finances through their control of the banks and currency. Small and new businesses needed more money in circulation to survive and grow, but Wall Street refused to permit this.

A "tight money" policy gave them bigger profits in higher interest rates, and' kept down competition to monopolies they controlled.

Big business refused to listen when Wifeon warned, "Capital must give over its too great preoccupation with the business of making those who control it individually rich, and must study to serve the interests of the people as a whole."

So Wilson proposed, and Congress passed, the Federal Reserve (Owen-Glass) Act that had far-reaching effects on the economy of the country. It set up a Federal Reserve Board with bank branches in twelve key cities throughout the nation. That broke Wall Street's monopoly by providing a dozen money centers where only one had existed before.

The new law also created a flexible currency to meet the needs of business. Our government today depends heavily upon this function of the Federal Reserve Board, both to keep us out of a depression and to prevent dangerous inflation that could send the price of bread soaring to a dollar or even higher.

Depression is a danger when the economy is stagnant, with unemployment growing. To create more jobs, the Federal Reserve Board indirectly makes more money available as loans to establish new businesses or expand old ones. Inflation is a danger when the economy is booming too fast, with too much money in circulation and prices soaring. The Board then shrinks the amount of money available for loans until the danger of inflation is past.

The Federal Bank Act of 1791 kept our nation out of bankruptcy in its infancy, gave it the power to grow, and widened legislative powers under the Constitution. The 16th Amendment that began income taxes in 1913 tried to apportion the costs of government fairly among all citizens. The Federal Reserve Act of 1913 has become a powerful weapon for keeping our nation prosperous while curbing inflation. And the Glass-Steagall Act of 1933 has made it safe for Americans to keep their savings in banks, without fear of bank failures.

Few financial laws have affected our lives more.

3
Laws that Protected Our Freedoms

The hall of a great Midwestern university buzzed with curiosity. It was filled with students majoring in political science, who had been asked to fill in "a questionnaire of your opinions." No one knew just what the quiz was all about.

After the results of the questionnaire had been tabulated, a group of amazed and chagrined professors listened as the head of the Department of Political Science spoke: "Gentlemen," he said, "about half of the students you have been teaching do *not* believe in the right of all Americans to assemble peaceably to complain against the government. They do *not* believe in the right of every accused person to be faced with his accuser, and have the chance to cross examine him. They do *not* believe in the right of an accused person not to have to testify against himself."

"Great Scott!" groaned one professor. "My students?"

"You may well clutch your heads in dismay, gentlemen. No less than 100 per cent of the students answered that they believed completely in the Bill of Rights. But the answers of half show that they haven't the foggiest notion of what the Bill of Rights is! And yet we are going to graduate these students with degrees in political science!"

Commenting on this revealing incident, Edward Bennett Williams, the nation's most distinguished attorney in the defense of personal and civil liberties, declared, "The average civics student in an American high school doesn't know what you are talking about if you refer to the basic guarantees of the Bill of Rights. The average college student is similarly ignorant."

This is a dangerous state of affairs. If the average American does not know or understand the laws that protect him and his fellow citizens, how can he sit on a jury—as he is required to do as a citizen—and reach a just decision in cases involving violations of the Bill of Rights? If he is the one arrested, how can he be sure of a fair trial himself?

Consider that not long ago a man in a New England city got up on a stepladder and made what sounded to police of that city like a dangerous radical speech. He was arrested and booked on charges of "inciting to riot." The man was a college professor. The "dangerous radical speech" with which he had been "inciting to riot" turned out to be the Bill of Rights itself. The police had arrested a man for reading aloud part of the Constitution of the United States!

No one knew better than the Founding Fathers of our nation how vitally important the Bill of Rights was to Amercans. When the Constitution was offered without these protections of freedom, Thomas Tredwell cried out in protest:

"Here we find no security for the rights of individuals . . . no bill of rights, no proper restriction of power. Our lives, our property, and our consciences are left wholly at the mercy of the legislature. . . . Is this, sir, a government for freemen? Are we thus to be duped out of our liberties?"

He compared a government to a mad horse that occasionally tries to run away with its rider. "Would he not, therefore, justly be deemed a madman, and deserve to have his neck broken, who should trust himself on this horse without any bridle at all?"

Thomas Jefferson was just as blunt in a letter to James Madison: "A bill of rights is what the people are entitled to against every government on earth, general or particular: and what no just government should refuse."

Their angry protests stirred up widespread public criticism. To pacify this outcry and obtain ratification of the Constitution itself, its defenders had to promise a Bill of Rights to protect the citizens against the government. That bill consisted of a series of amendments, the first ten of which were known as the Bill of Rights and became part of the Constitution eighteen months later in 1791.

The Bill of Rights was not a brand-new idea. The freedoms and rights it spells out derive from the Magna Carta of 1215, the first great document of human liberty which protected British freemen against the tyranny of authority.

The First Amendment, in some measure the most important one, guarantees to every citizen the freedom of religion, speech, and press, and the right to gather in groups "and to petition the government for a redress of grievances." Supreme Court Justice Hugo Black called the First Amendment "the heart of our Government."

It is the First Amendment that in recent times has given citizens the right to stage mass protests against the war in Vietnam, against nuclear warfare, against American foreign policy, against racial discrimination, against the draft. If the government tried to stop these protests, or arrest those who were protesting peacefully, the Supreme Court would find that the rights of these citizens under the First Amendment had been violated.

No matter how unpopular the views of a person or group may be, they have a constitutional right to advocate those views publicly. Their opponents have the same rights. If the government is allowed to deny freedom of speech, demonstration, press, or religion to any one group, then no group's freedoms are safe. This is why the Civil Liberties Union fights for anyone—Communist, Fascist, or vegetarian—who finds himself deprived of his rights under the First Amendment.

Citizens who considered certain state laws in violation of their rights under the First Amendment have gone to the Supreme Court, and have been upheld in important decisions affecting the whole nation. In 1941, for example, the Supreme Court set aside any state law that required school children to salute the American flag. This law violated the religious rights of some sects whose teachings did not allow them to salute any flag.

More recently the Supreme Court banned the official use of prayers and Bible reading in public schools to protect the rights of nonbelievers, as well as those who practiced different rituals. The place of religion, the Court indicated, was not in public schools but in church and in the home.

The First Amendment protects companies as well as individuals. In 1935 a group of nine Louisiana newspaper publishers tried to expose the corrupt practices of the Huey Long political machine that ran the state. The Louisiana legislature punished them by levying a tax so worded that it applied only to their newspapers but not to those supporting the Long machine. The Supreme Court threw out the tax as a violation of freedom of the press under the First Amendment.

In February, 1966, the Soviet government sentenced two of its authors to five to seven years at hard labor in Siberia for writing books critical of the Soviet regime. There is no First Amendment in the Soviet constitution.

In this same month a U.S. draft board reclassified almost two dozen college students as "1-A"—subject to immediate call-up—because they had demonstrated against the war in Vietnam, The Civil Liberties Union and many other organizations protested vigorously that these students were being punished for political opinions. Orders sped out from Washington, and the students were given back their "2-S"—student deferment—classification. There *is* a First Amendment in the American Constitution.

The next important amendment in the Bill of Rights is the Fourth—"the right of the people to be secure in their persons, houses, papers, and effects, against unreasonable searches and seizures." To make a legal search and seizure, police must first obtain a warrant from a judge, on the basis of sworn evidence showing reasonable justification.

The vital importance of the Fourth Amendment stems from the British concept that "an Englishman's home is his castle." Every citizen of a nation has a right to feel secure in his own home. The Fourth Amendment says he doesn't have to admit anyone who can't show a legal warrant from a court.

Law enforcement agencies often blinked at that law, illegally seizing evidence to prove the guilt of a suspect. They did not seek warrants beforehand because they did not have enough clear evidence to convince a court to issue one.

A key case, *Mapp v. Ohio,* reached the Supreme Court in 1961. The Court held that no state may convict a defendant if the evidence presented against him has been illegally obtained, even if the evidence proves his guilt. In the eyes of the Court, the protection of a citizen's rights under the Fourth Amendment is far more important than the conviction of a guilty wrongdoer who might be uncovered by an illegal raid.

Americans seldom appreciate how precious the Fourth Amendment is for the protection of their liberties. Under Hitler's Germany and Stalin's Russia, secret police constantly made midnight raids on citizens' homes, ransacked them and made arrests. Arrests were tantamount to conviction leading to prison or a death sentence.

The Fourth Amendment is your guarantee that this can't happen here.

The Fifth Amendment protects your rights as an individual. You cannot be deprived of life, liberty, or property except by due process of law, If you are tried at court and found innocent, you cannot be tried again for the same crime. Nor can you be compelled in any criminal case to give testimony against yourself.

This latter clause has become popularly known as "taking the Fifth." It is heard most often in connection with witnesses called before a congressional investigating committee who decline to answer questions, claiming immunity under their rights as defined by the Fifth Amendment.

"Taking the Fifth" is not an admission of guilt, nor can it be so considered. Undoubtedly some witnesses who exercise this right are guilty of violations they do not wish to reveal. But others are highly respectable citizens who refuse to answer on principle.

In 1956 the New York City Board of Education fired a teacher who invoked the Fifth Amendment at a hearing. He sued the Board. The Supreme Court ruled that no city employee could be dismissed for exercising his constitutional right.

The Sixth, Seventh, and Eighth Amendments spell out the rights of every person who is accused of a crime. The Sixth Amendment guarantees him a speedy public trial by jury, with the right to have a lawyer, call witnesses in his defense, and cross-examine witnesses against him.

In 1963 the Supreme Court received an amazing document—a handwritten petition from Clarence E. Gideon, a petty gambler and four-times-convicted felon jailed in Florida state prison for burglary. He claimed that because he had been too poor to afford a lawyer, he had been denied counsel at his trial, a violation of his rights under the Constitution.

The Court appointed Washington lawyer Abe Fortas (later made a Supreme Court Justice himself) to represent him. After hearing Fortas's arguments, the Supreme Court ruled in Gideon's favor, stating that under the Sixth Amendment every defendant was entitled to legal counsel which the state, if necessary, was obligated to provide free.

Thousands of prisoners who had been sent to jail without lawyers to defend them promptly filed petitions for new trials.

In 1966 the Supreme Court also set aside a conviction of murder because police had extorted a confession without first advising the defendant of his right to consult a lawyer.

These new rulings on the Sixth Amendment make it more difficult for the police to obtain convictions. But they also give Americans—poor members of minority groups especially—the full protection promised them in the Bill of Rights.

The Seventh Amendment guarantees the right of trial by jury in any civil suit involving a claim of more than $20. The Eighth Amendment guarantees protection against excessive bail (which could keep a poor man in jail until his trial), and against excessive fines or cruel and unusual punishment.

The Bill of Rights never assumes more importance than in times of war hysteria, when the military may attempt to exert powerful pressure against dissenters. The Supreme Court is ever on guard to protect the right of civilians to trial by jury, not by a military court.

In 1866 the Army arrested a civilian named Milligan on charges of subversion, tried him by a military commission, and condemned him to hang. On appeal, the Supreme Court ruled that military tribunals have no right to try civilians as long as civil courts are open and functioning, even though the nation is at war.

The issue came up again after the attack on Pearl Harbor, when the Army court-martialed civilians in Hawaii, and claimed the war as justification. The Court set aside the claim of the military, Justice Frank Murphy calling their trials "forbidden by the Bill of Rights." He added, "The right to jury trial and the other Constitutional rights of an accused individual are too fundamental to be sacrificed merely through a reasonable fear of military assault."

The Supreme Court has not been perfect in its wartime defense of American freedoms under the Bill of Rights. In February, 1942, thousands of Japanese-Americans in California were removed from their homes by order of the President, for fear that they would aid the Japanese enemy. Despite their bitter protests at this violation of their civil rights, they were interned at an inland relocation center.

The Supreme Court ruled the internment was constitutional under war conditions.

In 1870 another vital amendment was added to the Constitution to broaden and protect American freedoms—the Fifteenth. This new law spelled out, for the first time, the right of every American male, regardless of race, color or previous slavery, to vote. Its purpose in 1870 was to assure the Negro of equal rights in everyday affairs. Its impact on the Negro people, and the ways in which the South eventually made the law a "dead letter" for almost a century, will be discussed in a later chapter.

But the greater significance of the Fifteenth Amendment was that it established the principle of "one man—one vote" as the basis of elections in America. In a world of few democracies, it once more called attention to the United States as a nation governed directly by the will of the people.

Half the American people, however, still challenged that assumption as untrue: the half who wore skirts. Women grew increasingly outraged that men of all colors and races had the right of ballot, while they—many of them descendants of the original founders of the nation—were denied the vote.

The Women's Rights Convention, held at Seneca Falls, N.Y., in 1848, was the first to demand that women be given the ballot. Crusading Horace Greeley, famous fighting journalist of the New York *Tribune,* was one of the few male editors who dared to champion the cause of woman suffrage. Constant agitation by suffragettes like Susan B. Anthony, Elizabeth Cady Stanton, Ann Howard Shaw, Lucretia Mott, Carrie Chapman Catt, and Margaret Fuller finally brought about the Nineteenth Amendment in 1920, granting women the right to vote.

The laws that protected our freedoms had another effect as well. By safeguarding citizens from persecution or punishment for speaking and writing as they thought, these laws helped to develop a society of wonderfully diverse ideas. Many of these ideas, considered radical and daring when they were first expressed, later became incorporated in American laws.

Had the men who first dared to write or speak out boldly in the nineteenth century not been protected by the Bill of Rights, they might have been jailed and their ideas suppressed. Instead, thanks to the wisdom of the Founding Fathers, they were allowed to contribute the riches of their original minds to the national good.

And in the twentieth century, Presidents like Theodore Roosevelt, Woodrow Wilson, Franklin D. Roosevelt, John F. Kennedy, and Lyndon Johnson—all reformers—acted on those ideas to introduce social reforms that now benefit us all.

The process is still going on. In a turbulent and fast-changing world, application of the Bill of Rights to the burning issues of the 1960's, 1970's, and 1980's is, and will continue to be, as important as any time in our history.

4

The Red-White-
And-Blue Laws

In 1954 one man had the whole nation in an uproar. Millions of Americans stayed home from work to watch him roar, rant, and accuse in congressional hearings that were broadcast over TV networks throughout the entire day.

"The year," President Eisenhower wrote later, "began with Senator McCarthy riding high and ended with his being practically a political cipher." The President added, "His methods were frequently such as to arouse the resentment and opposition of informed Americans."

But many Americans had *not* been informed at the time Senator Joseph McCarthy of Wisconsin rose to power and prominence. They were frightened by the cold war, and by charges that the U.S. State Department was "riddled with Communists." In this atmosphere of fear and suspicion, McCarthy denounced prominent Democrats and liberals as "pinkos" and "fellow travelers."

As the new chairman of the Permanent Investigations Subcommittee of the Senate Committee on Governmental Operations, he used fake charges, accusations, false evidence, and appeals to prejudice to slander leading Americans, under the protection of congressional immunity to lawsuits. Some objects of his attacks Included Dwight D. Eisenhower, Senator

Millard Tydings, General George Marshall, Presidents Roosevelt and Truman, Adlai Stevenson, and America's poet laureate, Archibald MacLeish.

Attacking Dr. Pusey, President of Harvard, McCarthy charged that Harvard was a "sanctuary for Commos." He claimed that the State Department was harboring 205 Communists. When the FBI investigated, the charge was found to be groundless. McCarthy then roared that "the Commies" had destroyed the evidence. He went on to attack Protestant churches, American embassies abroad, the Voice of America, and finally the United States Army itself, as "Communist-infiltrated."

Red-white-and-blue organizations of self-appointed "superpatriots" rallied behind McCarthy's banner. They demanded that cities, states, universities, and corporations follow McCarthy's example and probe the "loyalty" of employees. At least ten thousand Americans were dismissed from their jobs on unsubstantial evidence. When witnesses refused to submit to McCarthy's grilling, citing the Fifth Amendment of the Bill of Rights, he insisted that this proved they were guilty.

In this atmosphere, the 1954 Congress passed a law requiring revocation of American citizenship for persons convicted of conspiracy, and authorizing the death penalty in cases of peacetime espionage.

The full meaning of McCarthyism was forcibly brought home to the American people for the first time in the televised hearings of his charges against the United States Army. Until then, reported the American Institute of Public Opinion, an incredible 50 per cent of the American people had generally supported McCarthy. Now, suddenly, they were able to witness his bullying, arrogant accusations and fantastic charges.

Counsel for the Army, Joseph Welch, became a national hero when he quietly said, in front of twenty million watching Americans, "If it were in my power to forgive you for your reckless cruelty, I would do so. I like to think that I am a gentle man, but your forgiveness will have to come from someone other than me. . . . Have you no sense of decency, sir?"

With President Eisenhower's approval, a Senate committee recommended censure of McCarthy for conduct unbecoming a member of the Senate that tended to bring Congress into disrepute. This resolution passed the Senate by a three-to-one vote. A new poll showed that the public's support of McCarthy had dropped sharply; he was now recognized as a dangerous demagogue. The four-year McCarthy era of red-white-and-blue hysteria was over at last, and the nation slowly recovered from McCarthyism.

But how had it happened in the first place?

The rise of McCarthyism had its origins in the history of the nation's red-white-and-blue laws, and the persistence of what author James Baldwin calls "the American vice—prejudice and intolerance."

For many decades America was a celebrated haven for the oppressed people of other lands. Beneath the Statue of Liberty these beautiful words are inscribed:

Give me your tired, your poor,
Your huddled masses yearning to breathe free.
The wretched refuse of your teeming shore.
Send these, the homeless, tempest-tost to me,
I lift my lamp beside the golden door.

But immigrants were never quite as welcome as this poem by Emma Lazarus suggests. Throughout American history there has always been a large and powerful segment of American opinion which persisted in viewing "alien" and "sedition" as opposite sides of the same coin.

In his Farewell Address of 1798, Washington warned his countrymen, "History and experience prove that foreign-influence is one of the most baneful foes of republican government." He feared that America's political parties, one sympathizing with France and the other with Britain, would in this conflict destroy the unity of the young nation.

In 1798 a series of sea skirmishes between the American and French navies led Alexander Hamilton and his anti-French Federalists to advocate war against France. As diplomatic relations between France and America grew chilly, and war seemed likely, a Federalist-dominated Congress passed the Alien and Sedition Acts of 1798.

The Naturalization Act extended from five to fourteen years the residence requirement for citizenship. The Alien Act gave the President power for two years to order any dangerous alien out of the country. The Alien Enemies Act provided that, in time of war, aliens might be deported or imprisoned for as long as the President decreed. The Sedition Act made it a criminal offense to foster opposition to United States laws; to aid a foreign power in an anti-American plot; or to circulate "false, scandalous and malicious" criticism of the government or its officers. Hamilton talked a hesitant President John Adams into signing these acts into law.

A wave of violent resentment and indignation swept the country. The Democratic-Republican Party of Jefferson and Madison saw the acts as a political trick to destroy the influence of French immigrants and French sympathizers, as well as to stifle criticism of Federalist policies by the Democratic-Republicans. In addition, many Americans were, or recently had been, "aliens," and some wished to bring their families to join them.

Jefferson and Madison charged that the Federalists were concentrating dangerous power in the national government, and that the Alien and Sedition Acts were a gross infringement of personal and civil liberties as guaranteed in the Bill of Rights. They drafted the Virginia and Kentucky Resolutions, adopted by those states, affirming states' rights to nullify within their own boundaries any federal law that "assumes undelegated powers."

When Jefferson succeeded Adams as President in 1802, he lost no time in getting Congress to repeal the Naturalization Act, reducing the fourteen years' residence required for citizenship back to five.

In 1918, under President James Monroe, Congress passed its first act regulating immigration, requiring ships' captains to provide descriptive lists of passengers docking in American ports. An annual average of 400,000 immigrants was arriving in Manhattan by 1855. During the Civil War, with a labor shortage caused by millions of Americans in uniform, Lincoln asked Congress to establish a system to encourage immigration. The Immigration Act of 1846 allowed employers to import aliens for contract labor under regulations set up by a Commissioner of Immigration.

All through the latter half of the nineteenth century a steadily increasing stream of immigrants arrived on American shores to build the railroads, open the West, and fill the factories. In 1882, following a year of bad crops, inflated prices, and strikes for higher wages in President Chester Arthur's administration, workers were angered by the use of cheap Chinese labor. Their national union, the Knights of Labor, pressured Congress into passing the first Chinese Exclusion Act, barring Chinese laborers from entering the United States. Later that year Congress passed the first act restricting general immigration.

Fighting for better working conditions, with strikes for higher wages and shorter hours, the Knights of Labor were hostile to new immigrants, viewing them as a threat to native workers. An indication of the temper of the times was the lynching by an angry New Orleans mob in 1891 of eleven Italian immigrants jailed for "lawlessness."

In 1894 an act of Congress set up the Bureau of Immigration. The flood of immigration, despite restrictive laws, reached a new high tide in 1907 with a record 1,285,349 aliens arriving in America that year. Congress rushed a new Immigration Act excluding "undesirables," and raised the head tax to $4.00 apiece to keep down the number of unskilled laborers arriving under their own steam.

English-speaking Americans grew increasingly annoyed at the extent to which foreign tongues were heard in the cities and in Midwestern farming communities. They were also irritated by the manners and customs of Old World immigrants. The outbreak of World War I in 1914 led to a steady rise of anti-German feeling which American superpatriots soon inflamed into a cult of rabidly nationalistic prejudice.

One group calling themselves the National Security League invaded movie theaters and harangued audiences with speeches designed to arouse anti-German emotions. The government censored mail from Germany, and the German language was removed from college curricula. In 1916 the famous Black Tom explosion occurred at munitions docks in Jersey City, killing two and causing damages of $22,000,000. Traced to German saboteurs, It sent anti-German feeling soaring to fever pitch. Vigilantes smeared yellow paint on the houses of anyone suspected of not having sentiments they considered red-white-and-blue enough. Now Congress passed, over President Woodrow Wilson's veto, an immigration bill compelling immigrants to take a literacy test. This unfair bill had been vetoed by two former Presidents—Cleveland who called it in 1897 "a radical departure from our natural policy," and Taft in 1913. Fears that Central America might aid Germany in a war against the United States led Congress to pass a more liberal law in 1917, the Jones Act, granting citizenship and suffrage to Puerto Ricans.

When America finally did declare war on Germany, Congress promptly passed the Espionage Act, which imposed heavy fines (up to $10,000 and twenty years in jail) for aiding enemies in time of war by obstructing the draft, spreading false reports, or interfering with military action. This act was amended in May, 1918, by the Sedition Act, which provided penalties for bringing into "contempt, scorn, contumely or disrespect," by speech or publication, the Amercan form of government, armed forces, flag or uniform. Several hundred pacifists and Socialists were imprisoned under this law, which they regarded as an unconstitutional revalidation of the Federalists' old Sedition Act of 1798.

It is significant that the Sedition Act of 1918 followed by only six months the October Revolution which established the Bolsheviks in power in Russia. This event made dominant classes in America and Europe nervous, fearing a labor-led revolutionary upheaval in the West following the end of the war. They attacked social, economic, and labor unrest in America as Bolshevist-inspired.

Between 1919 and 1920 a conservative Congress considered no less than seventy bills dealing with "unlawful discussion," aliens, denaturalization of citizens, and other expressions of upper-class fear. Most of these measures were instigated by Attorney General A. Mitchell Palmer, after thirty-six bombs were mailed by unidentified persons to government officials and business tycoons, Palmer among them. Alarmed by all dissenters and aliens, Palmer insisted that the Communists were ready to "destroy the government at one fell swoop."

From 1919 to 1921 he led a repressive, punitive campaign historians later labeled the "Red Scare." He deported 249 Russian immigrants who had been accused of no crime. Three hundred congressmen were charged with "disloyalty." Yale was attacked for permitting some professors to speak out against Palmer; and teachers were forced to sign "loyalty oaths." In West Virginia 150 alleged members of the IWW—the left-wing "Wobblies"—were forced to kiss the flag, then deported. On New Year's Day, 1920, Palmer's spies and agents arrested 6,000 people, mostly ignorant aliens with no understanding of the charges made against them; some were jailed, others deported.

To silence a growing tide of protest, Palmer released figures suggesting that up to 25 per cent of Americans were suspect as members of the "Bolshevik plot." He even caused five elected members of the New York State Legislature to be denied seats because they were members of the Socialist Party. This was too much for the distinguished Supreme Court justice, Charles Evans Hughes. Then Secretary of State under President Harding, Hughes defended the New York Socialists, and led public opinion in demanding and obtaining wholesale cancellation of deportation warrants.

This brought about the downfall of Palmerism, which had occurred largely because Wilson, seriously ill since September, 1919, had left the country's affairs without national leadership. And the Sedition Act of May, 1918, had given Palmer the club of legality that he used against America's workers, aliens, liberals, nonconformists, radicals, Socialists and teachers. His like was not seen again until McCarthy repeated his tactics in the 1950's,

The case of *Gitlow v. People of N.Y.* in 1925 raised further doubt of the constitutionality of any sedition act. The Supreme Court upheld a New York State Supreme Court ruling in favor of the right of "radicals to preach revolutionary doctrines."

The United States changed its immigration policy again after World War I. By the year 1921 it began to seem as though all of Europe was trying to move to America to escape from the war-ravaged continent. Congress hastily passed an Emergency Quota Act restricting immigration for any European country to 3 per cent of its nationals living here in 1910.

The Immigration Act of 1924 reduced this quota further to 2 per cent of those resident in 1890, discriminating against the people who were not largely Anglo-Saxon.

Unreasonable fear of aliens began to seize Congress in 1939 when Europe was again at war.

"In this atmosphere of international fear and intrigue," related President Harry S. Truman, "it was natural that some demagogues would be tempted to make political capital out of the situation." Congressmen sought headlines by holding hearings marked by wild charges, false accusations, browbeating of witnesses. "People were being tried before a congressional committee instead of a court of law," Truman recalled. "This was a dangerous misuse of the investigatory powers of Congress."

In 1940 this Congress passed the Smith Act, which required registration and fingerprinting of aliens, and forbade any person to advocate overthrowing the government by force, or knowingly to belong to any group that advocated it. In 1951 the Supreme Court upheld the act in the case of eleven convicted Communist Party leaders on the ground that the "Communist conspiracy created a clear and present danger."

But in 1957 the Supreme Court ruled that party membership alone was not sufficient for conviction under the act, unless a member *personally* urged violent revolution.

Laws like the Smith Act were important, not only to Communists or other extreme radical groups, but also to all Americans. They attempted to define the limits to which critics could go in disagreeing with the government. Most Americans agreed with the Smith Act that advocating overthrow of the government by force was going too far and should be considered a criminal act punishable by a jail sentence.

Yet one famous and respected American had said, "Whenever they [the American people] shall grow weary of their existing Government, they can exercise their constitutional right of amending it, or their revolutionary right to dismember and overthrow it." The American who, under the Smith Act, could have been prosecuted and sent to jail for saying that in his First Inaugural Address on March 4, 1861, was Abraham Lincoln.

In 1948 the House Committee on the Un-American Activities (HUAC), under chairman J. Parnell Thomas, opened loyalty investigations without regard for civil rights. President Truman charged that even when a man was cleared, the dossier was kept intact and available for blacklisting, making it impossible for him to find employment.

In 1949, eleven Communist Party members were convicted of violating the Smith Act after a nine-month trial, ten of them receiving five-year sentences. Following the outbreak of the Korean War in 1950, a new wave of anti-Communist sentiment swept the country. Congress passed the McCarran Internal Security Act, requiring registration of Communists and "Communist-Front organizations," providing for deportation of Communist immigrants; and prohibiting immigration of anyone who had been a member of a "totalitarian organization." The Subversive Activities Control Act of 1950 further enjoined any person who would *probably* engage in activities against the United States from registering under this act. Both these acts, reminiscent of the old Sedition Act under which the Palmer raids had taken place, were denounced and vetoed by President Truman.

In 1952, HUAC began to hint about "subversion" at Yale, just as Palmer had done, and a Yale alumni committee was forced to investigate and report that they found no evidence to this effect. Once more college professors from coast to coast became afraid to say or write anything controversial.

In 1952 the McCarran-Walter Act (also passed over President Truman's veto) revised the immigration laws again. Further restrictions were placed on the immigration or naturalization of

Communists or "Communist sympathizers." Immigration quotas were reduced sharply.

The red-white-and-blue hysteria rose to fever pitch with McCarthy. With the passing of McCarthyism, the basic early American tradition of tolerance slowly reasserted itself.

In 1953 a Presidential Committee on Immigration and Naturalization urged revisions in the McCarran-Walter Act. The Congress liberalized immigration provisions in a series of subsequent Acts. A new Refugee Relief Act authorized admission of 214,000 refugees in excess of regular quotas.

In 1957 special legislation permitted over 27,000 Hungarian refugees to enter the United States on an emergency basis.

At the foot of the Statue of Liberty, on October 3, 1965, President Lyndon Johnson signed a radical new immigration bill that finally did away with the old 1924 quota system based on national origins that had kept many south Europeans waiting for as long as ten years for admission under their nations' quotas.

The new immigration law, effective July 1, 1968, admits an annual average of 350,000 immigrants a year on a basis of "first come, first served." Preference is given on a basis of skills and family relationships. The old law, the President charged, was "incompatible with our basic American tradition of asking not where a person comes from, but what are his personal qualities." The new law sets no quotas for any individual nation, but limits total immigration from Western Hemisphere nations to 120,000 a year, and any other individual nation to 20,000 a year.

America's former immigration laws favored white, Anglo-Saxon nations. They largely excluded colored, Mediterranean, Middle East, and Oriental populations—who make up the vast bulk of the world's people. This prejudiced policy has hurt America's image abroad. It will take time before the new Johnson immigration law convinces the world that the words inscribed beneath the Statue of Liberty are sincere.

There are also fresh winds blowing in American thought about the reckless use of alien and sedition laws that have so often violated the spirit and letter of the Bill of Rights.

"Without open minds," said the late Justice of the Supreme Court Felix Frankfurter, "there can be no open society. The Smith Act is unconstitutional on its face . . . a virulent form of prior censorship."

In *Functions and Policies of American Government,* Professor Lawrence Herson of Ohio State University declares, "Our anti-subversion laws . . . have spelled an end to free speech in certain areas of discussion. While few question the need to suppress Communism, many rest uneasy at the thought of defining to the point of extinction any aspect of free speech or freedom of political association."

President Truman wrote in his memoirs, "To enforce the Sedition Laws, the Bill of Rights had to be thrown out the window. When sanity returned, most of the bills which had not expired were repealed. Later, in 1919, there was the period in which A. Mitchell Palmer, as Attorney General, used the forces of government in raids on many citizens. It was a terrible thing. That was the 'Communist hysteria' program of its day. During other periods of hysteria, attacks on the rights of individuals were made on other pretexts in total disregard of guarantees under the Bill of Rights. But we recovered from all of them."

In 1966, when the Senate Foreign Relations Committee criticized American foreign policy in Vietnam and the Dominican Republic as a tragic mistake, many angry voices cried out once more that such criticism was "dangerous treason" and should be silenced.

5

Laws that Shaped Our Foreign Policy

Captain James Barron of the United States frigate *Chesapeake* had no reason to feel alarmed when the larger British frigate *Leopard* hailed him near Cape Henry one sunny June morning in 1807.

"Stand to!" shouted the British captain. "I am sending a boarding party to your vessel!"

Barron looked puzzled. "What is your reason, sir?"

"Reason enough! There are British seamen aboard your frigate, deserters from His Majesty's Navy!"

"That is a matter for diplomats, sir, not sea captains. I will not permit you to board."

The *Leopard,* which had fifty guns to the *Chesapeake's* thirty-six, promptly opened fire. In the first broadside twenty-one American sailors were killed or wounded, and the *Chesapeake* received a heavy shot through her mainmast and had her main-royal yard shot away. Outmatched in armor and speed, Barron submitted.

The British boarded the American vessel, searched her thoroughly, and took off four men. Only one was a British deserter; the other three were American seamen. Hand-cuffed, they were driven by bayonets into the *Leopard's* filthy dungon, where they were kept for forty days until the frigate returned to Falmouth. This was the first of a series of outrages committed against American sovereignty by the British Navy.

In his Farewell Address, Washington had warned Americans against getting involved in Europe's quarrels. Now his warning was being sharply underscored by the search-and-seizure tactics of an England fighting France in the Napoleonic Wars. President Thomas Jefferson felt that it had become urgent to spell out America's policy of neutrality.

In December, 1807, Congress passed the Embargo Act, prohibiting all ships from leaving the United States for foreign ports. When this drastic act almost ruined American shipping and crippled the economy, it was replaced in March, 1809, by the Non-Intercourse Act, denying trade only to England and France, but allowing it to all other nations. When France promised to respect American neutrality, the law was amended to apply only against Britain.

The neutrality laws of 1807–1810 thus ironically led to a rapidly worsening relationship between England and America, bringing on the War of 1812. But for over a century the American people insisted upon following Washington's advice: "The great rule of conduct for us, in regard to foreign nations is, in extending our commercial relations, to have with them as little political connection as possible."

Neutrality laws were relied upon for this purpose. But just as they led to the War of 1812, they also led to America's subsequent involvement in two world wars. Only after long and painful experience did the American people learn that they could not insulate themselves from the rest of the world, even though they were protected by two great oceans.

Strong anti-European feeling led Congress to pass the high protective tariff bill of 1816, designed to shut European manufactures out of the American market. The plan was to protect home industries, give them a chance to grow, and make the nation economically independent of Europe.

The South soon grew disenchanted with this economic foreign policy. The industrial North thrived. But the South was forced to pay higher prices for everything it needed. And it was being drastically curtailed in the amount of cotton it could sell abroad because of "tit-for-tat" high tariffs in Europe.

The high-tariff policy of the United States persisted, nevertheless, from 1816 to 1934, with a brief nine-year intermission when Wilson introduced the Underwood Tariff of 1913. This low-tariff bill removed the import tax on food and other necessities of the average citizen, and reduced it on articles that no longer needed protection from foreign competition.

Wilson did not get his low-tariff policy without a fight. He accused big business of setting up a powerful lobby to crush the Underwood tariff: "It is of serious interest to the country that the people at large should have no lobby and be voiceless in these matters, while great bodies of astute men seek to create an artificial opinion and to overcome the interests of the public for their private profit."

In September, 1922, during the second year of Republican President Harding's administration, Congress once again restored protection for American business with the Fordney-McCumber Tariff.

Many of the milestones of American foreign policy were not set up by Congress but by the President. This has often been the cause of clashes between the two branches of government—the Executive and the Legislative. Often presidential proclamations have had the same effect as law, even though Congress had not legally passed them as bills.

In 1821, Tsar Alexander I of Russia insisted that his nation had the right to colonize the western coast of North America, and some European nations were considering a plan to restore former Spanish colonies in America to the Spanish crown. In his annual message to Congress on December 2, 1823, President James Monroe announced that the United States would not allow any European power to interfere with or colonize any part of both American continents. The Monroe Doctrine, though never actually a law, has remained a powerful cornerstone of American policy to the present day.

The growth of industrial capitalism forced changes in the insularity of the United States. By the 1890's American manufacturers were producing a vast surplus of products and needed overseas markets. They also needed to control sources of cheap raw materials they used. Powerful pressures began to be put on both Congress and the President to develop a new foreign policy that was openly imperialistic.

In 1890 Congress signaled the new attitude of America by passing a Naval Act to build naval forces strong enough to protect the United States in the Atlantic and to enforce our will in Latin America and the Pacific. In quick order, Samoa, Hawaii, the Philippines, Puerto Rico, and Guam fell under the American flag. The last three acquisitions were obtained by going to war with Spain in Cuba over the sinking of the U.S. battleship *Maine*.

As part of this new foreign policy, Secretary of State John Hay forced the European powers who were exploiting China commercially to give equal rights to the United States.

Fiercely resenting this "Open Door" policy of Western imperialism, a Chinese patriotic society known as the Boxers attacked the foreign settlement at Peking in 1900.

Presidential action, rather than laws by Congress, continued to guide American foreign policy under President Theodore Roosevelt, who advocated, "Speak softly but carry a big stick." A firm believer in dollar diplomacy—sending troops to secure and protect American investments and power—he overthrew the government of Panama to put through the canal project. During Theodore Roosevelt's administration, Cuba became an American satellite, essentially controlled by the American sugar industry, and United States Marines were landed in Honduras to protect American corporation property.

Woodrow Wilson's election in 1914 reversed the tide of an American foreign policy that was being run in the interests of big business. Once more the old tradition of "neutrality" guided the nation, ever more so as Europe plunged into a new war. Again, this policy was spelled out by presidential speeches rather than by legal bills passed by Congress.

But Wilson's desperate attempts to keep the nation out of war were doomed by Germany's persistent sinking of vessels carrying American citizens. Appealing at last to Congress on April 2, 1917, Wilson was given a war resolution by both Houses which enabled him to declare war on Germany.

When the war had been won, he asked Congress to ratify the Versailles Treaty, which committed America to become a member of the League of Nations. Congress refused, following the lead of Senator Henry Cabot Lodge. Most Americans were tired of war and its sacrifices. They wanted to forget Europe, and turn back to the nation's old isolationist policies. Congress also once more introduced a high protective tariff.

Thus America withdrew into its shell until the shock of the depression years, 1929–1933. Then, little by little, Americans began to realize that what happened to Londoners, Parisians, Berliners, and Milanese directly affected them, too.

In 1934 Congress passed the Trade Agreements Act, authorizing the President to enter into agreements with other nations willing to reduce their tariffs if we would reduce ours, by as much as 50 per cent. Within a few years reciprocal agreements brought the United States a vastly increased foreign trade.

In place of the old "big stick" policy in Latin America, so fiercely resented by nations south of the border, Franklin Roosevelt announced a "good neighbor policy." He ended our protectorate in Cuba, withdrew the Marines from Haiti, and promised the republics of Central and South America that the United States would never again intervene in their affairs. Under the Roosevelt administration, United States-Latin American relations became warm and cordial for the first time.

If Congress was finally willing to scrap America's high protective tariff in favor of trade agreements with Europe, it was still determined to stay out of the continent's political struggles. Hitler's rise to power in Germany made it ominously clear that war was coming again.

Many congressmen were embittered by the Nye investigation of 1934, which revealed that American munitions makers and financiers had made gigantic profits out of World War I. Some believed that these men had cynically put pressure on America to enter the war for their own greedy purposes.

Antiwar feeling ran high, both among the people and the Congress. From 1935 to 1937 Congress expressed this feeling in a series of three Neutrality Acts placing an embargo upon the export of arms to belligerent nations, denying them loans or credits, forbidding Americans to travel on their ships, and preventing the arming of American merchant vessels.

Once again, ironically, the Neutrality Acts worked against the interests of the American people, dragging them closer to war. In 1936 Loyalist Spain, a democracy, was fighting for its life against a Fascist uprising led by General Franco. He was supported with tanks, planes, and guns by Hitler and Mussolini, who were using Spain as a rehearsal of the major war they planned against the democracies. The Spanish government could get no help from America because of the neutrality acts. But Franco obtained all the munitions he needed from the

Axis powers, who could also buy from us as technical "nonbelligerents."

Spain's democratic government was crushed. Our failure to revoke the Neutrality Acts convinced Hitler that we would let him attack and swallow the democracies one by one. Thus emboldened, he unleashed full-scale war in Europe.

In January, 1939, a worried Roosevelt at last warned Congress that the Neutrality Acts "may actually give aid to an aggressor and deny it to the victim." Later that year Nazi Germany invaded Poland, forcing Poland's allies, England and France, to declare war. At last, in September, Congress met in special session and repealed the embargo provisions of the Neutrality Acts. Weeks later they passed a fourth Neutrality Act, authorizing the sale of munitions on a cash-and-carry basis.

However, it became clear early in 1941 that Great Britain was running out of funds and could no longer afford to pay for the arms it needed to fight off the German war machine.

Roosevelt appealed to the American people to renounce neutrality as a foreign policy.

"Suppose," he said, "my neighbor's house catches fire, and I have a length of garden hose four or five hundred feet away. If he can take my garden hose and connect it up with his hydrant, I may help him to put out his fire. Now, what do I do? I don't say to him before that operation, 'Neighbor, my garden hose cost me $15; you have to pay me $15 for it' . . . I don't want $15—I want my garden hose back before the fire is over."

Congress responded with the Lend-Lease Bill, which made it clear that America's sympathies were with Britain, and that we were determined to support the British people in their fight for survival. Roosevelt was given power to lend or lease American war materiel to "any country whose defense the President deems vital to the defense of the United States."

Roosevelt's "fire hose" kept England from perishing in the Nazi holocaust. By the end of the year the wisdom of Lend-Lease had proved itself. The Japanese attack on Pearl Harbor brought us into the war against the Axis powers. It was our ally England who helped us form one side of the nutcracker that finally crushed Hitler. The other side, the Soviet Union, was also aided in its struggle by the Lend-Lease Bill.

After the war it was finally clear to the American people that neutrality, insularity and isolation—the foreign policy of Washington we had clung to, and which had led us into two world wars—was hopelessly unrealistic for the twentieth century. Air power had shrunk the world. No nation alone was safe from the reach of a dictator bent on world conquest.

So Congress led the way to a new foreign policy. After World War I it had blocked Wilson's attempt to lead us into the League of Nations. But now it finally brought America into a world organization by passing the United Nations Participation Act in 1945. But the new UN was not strong enough to cope with urgent postwar problems.

No longer united by the war effort, the interests of the United States and the Soviet Union came into conflict. This new "cold war" convinced President Truman that Stalin intended to bring the war-stricken nations of western Europe under Communist influence or control. To prevent this, Truman asked Congress to approve a program of large-scale economic and military aid to nations he considered endangered.

The Truman Doctrine became the new American policy in May, 1947, when Congress passed the Greek-Turkish Aid Bill. The following spring it passed the Foreign Assistance Act of 1948, known as the Marshall Plan, to help sixteen countries of western Europe toward economic recovery. Finally, in 1949 Congress gave its approval to the North Atlantic Treaty Organization—NATO—a military alliance with western Europe aimed at a common defense against any possible act of Soviet aggression.

Thus in five swift years America rejected its former isolationist foreign policy, and staked its future safety on anti-Communist treaties and alliances with other nations. Now a world power, the United States was recognized as leader of the democracies.

In this role Truman felt that world peace depended heavily on winning neutral nations to the side of the democracies, or at least keeping them out of the Communist camp. But how?

Most of the uncommitted nations were "have-nots"—technically backward, undeveloped, the people often oppressed by a rich ruling class. These were conditions that favored the appeal of communism, not capitalist democracy. The neutrals, moreover, were deeply skeptical of the dollar diplomacy of the United States in Latin America and the colonialism of Britain and France in Africa and Asia.

Truman felt that we could win the friendship of the world's neutrals only by proving our willingness to help them with their problems, and by our ability to do a better job of it than either the Soviet Union or Red China could. So in 1949 he proposed a "Point Four" program of technical aid to help them improve their methods of production, food yield, health and education. The following year Congress voted to carry out this ambitious program through an International Development Fund.

In 1950 the cold war heated up to a shooting war in Korea when the North Koreans, spurred on by Stalin, invaded South Korea. The UN sent its forces, largely American, to the aid of the South Koreans. China entered the war on the side of the North Koreans, and the conflict seesawed back and forth until the new Republican President, Dwight Eisenhower, finally brought about an armistice in July, 1953.

John Foster Dulles, Eisenhower's Secretary of State, was convinced that America had to build a wall of anti-Communist power in the Pacific to contain Red China. He entered into a series of defensive alliances—primarily SEATO, in which eight Pacific powers agreed to come to the aid of those endangered by armed aggression; he also entered into a mutual defense treaty with Nationalist China. Congress enacted these policies into law in 1955.

Two years later Congress also passed a joint resolution endorsing the Eisenhower Doctrine—military and economic aid to Middle East nations to preserve their independence, and the use of American troops, if necessary, to resist Communist aggression in this area. In effect, for a dozen years following World War II, Congress obediently carried out a White House foreign policy of encircling the two great Communist powers—Russian and China—with a ring of military bases and treaties designed to keep their influence and borders from expanding.

But many senators were becoming alarmed at the way in which the White House was initiating foreign policy, then sending it to Congress for a rubber stamp of approval. The Constitution required the President to seek the *advice and consent* of the Senate, so that the people's representatives could have a voice in shaping policies that affected peace and war.

In 1953 Senator John Bricker, an Ohio Republican, introduced the Bricker Amendment to restrict the President's treaty-making powers, thus giving the Senate a greater voice in American foreign policy. The bill did not pass.

In 1966 the issue became explosive. America was becoming increasingly involved in the Vietnam War, and there was rising anxiety and protest about the nature of this involvement. Congress had never given its advice or consent to such a war. Senator William Fulbright, Chairman of the Senate Foreign Relations Committee, felt strongly that the American public should be fully informed of all arguments pro and con.

The Johnson administration was opposed to this, feeling that a great public debate would give Communist forces in Vietnam the impression that American support for the war was divided. Nevertheless, Fulbright went ahead with televised hearings that let the public hear expert testimony on all sides of American foreign policy in the Pacific. Millions of Americans grew critical of many facets of the government's tactics and objectives.

Under pressure of the Fulbright hearings, changes of policy began to develop. The "hawks" of the administration who wanted dangerous escalation of the Vietnam War were curbed. Urgent priority was given to a program of economic reforms for the South Vietnamese people. They were also promised free elections as soon as possible.* And the State Department reversed its policy of trying to keep Red China isolated.

The great Senate debate of 1966 helped to restore the prestige of the Senate in the field of foreign policy. President Johnson, and those who hope to follow him in the White House, were given notice that in the future the administration must *first* seek the advice and consent of the Senate before making crucial decisions involving peace and war.

---

* These elections were held in September of 1967.

6

Laws that Developed Our Resources

"River's rising!" a farmer's wife phoned in from the mountains of North Carolina.

"Headwaters approaching flood stage!" a woodsman phoned in from a pole in a Virginia forest.

Hundreds of reports came in from remote rain-gauge stations keeping track of the rapidly swelling tributaries of the huge Tennessee River. The people of the Tennessee Valley region had much to be anxious about. Only five years earlier a raging Mississippi River had surged over its banks, leaving a million people homeless in the Ohio and Mississippi valleys.

But even more was at stake that winter of 1942. America was at war, and in desperate need of the vital war plants working day and night at Chattanooga. If the Tennessee flooded, these essential industries would be forced to shut down under several feet of water. Apart from the costly damage, it might be weeks before full operation could be resumed. This catastrophe would be the equivalent of a major battle victory for Germany or Japan in America's desperate peril.

Fortunately for the nation, the reports from the rain gauge stations in 1942 were more than just a warning to people in the valley to flee to the hills, They were a part of a new control network begun nine years earlier—the Intelligence Service of the TVA, or Tennessee Valley Authority.

Sparked by the reports, TVA's central control office flashed orders to the various dams built throughout the valley to hold back the waters of tributaries, wherever there was a threat that these waters spilling into the Tennessee would add to the danger of a flood. Steel gates in the dams were lowered or raised by remote-control buttons.

Day by day the rate of water release from each tributary was precisely controlled until the crisis was over. The Tennessee never crested to flood stage; Chattanooga's war plants kept turning out the vital sinews that helped the nation defeat the Axis; hundreds of thousands of American defense workers and farmers were spared the miseries of a flood.

All because Congress passed a law in 1933.

Since America began as a nation two ideas have clashed constantly about the control and development of our natural resources. Champions of free enterprise insist that these should be privately owned and operated; that only this method will assure their most efficient development.

Champions of "big government," on the other hand, argue that a nation's natural resources belong to all the people, not to the few who lay claim to it. They feel that only the government is capable of using these resources for the benefit of all, operating for the public good rather than private profit.

As a result of this struggle for almost two centuries, government and private industry have compromised. In areas such as conservation, Congress has kept power in government hands. In others, such as raw materials, private enterprise largely exercises control. Where private business failed to build dams and supply power, the government has done so. Today both work as partners in aerospace and nuclear projects, with private businesses and universities doing research, development, and construction under government subsidies.

The right of the federal government to direct and pay for internal developments first came under fire in 1820, when Congress passed the Maysville Bill and sent it to the White House for the President's signature. The bill provided funds for a road to be built in Kentucky from Maysville to Lexington.

President Jackson vetoed the bill, declaring sharply that the federal government had no constitutional power to subsidize local roads, canals, or any other internal improvements within a single state.

Throughout much of the nineteenth century, lumbering was a major industry in the United States, and timber one of the most vital resources. In a nation with vast forests, no one was concerned about letting the lumber companies cut and sell as much timber as the market called for. But when the immense forests of the Great Lakes began to disappear, it suddenly began to dawn on Congress that trees were not inexhaustible.

In 1891 Congress finally passed the Forest Reserves Act, authorizing the President to reserve large sections of public lands for national forest preserves. This bill marked the beginning of the conservation policy in America. Soon afterward President Theodore Roosevelt gave vigorous support to conservation by setting aside 148 million acres as timber reserves, and emphasized the importance of using them as national parks of great natural beauty.

Roosevelt also sponsored the Newlands Reclamation Act of 1902, passed by Congress, authorizing the use of money from the sale of public land for the construction of irrigation projects to reclaim arid lands. Fifty years later, thanks to the Newlands Act, farmers in seventeen states were enjoying the use of over seven million fertile acres that had once been useless. And the 241 public dams that had made this possible were also providing

Americans in those regions with cheap electric power and flood control.

Conservation became the twentieth-century American way of life in 1907, when Theodore Roosevelt sent his Seventh Annual Message to Congress. "The conservation of our natural resources and their proper use constitute the fundamental problem which underlies almost every other problem of our national life," he said. " . . . The government has been endeavoring to get our people to look ahead and to substitute a planned and orderly development of our resources in place of a haphazard striving for immediate profit."

He explained: "Utilization of waterways and water-power, forestry, irrigation, and the reclamation of lands threatened with overflow, are all interdependent parts of the same problem." And he warned, "We are prone to speak of the resources of this country as inexhaustible; this is not so. . . . If the consumption and growth continue unchanged, practically all our lumber will be exhausted in another generation."

It was not the conservation policy, however, but World War I that led to the construction of a dam that stirred up a hornet's nest of controversy. In order to provide power for the manufacture of explosives and nitrates needed for the war effort, Congress authorized President Wilson to build the Muscle Shoals dam on the Tennessee River. The dam's hydroelectric station produced far more power than was needed for the purpose.

In 1928 Congress passed, another bill setting up a government-owned corporation to sell this surplus power. Privately-owned public utilities in the Tennessee Valley vigorously protested the federal government's intention to compete with them in the sale of electricity. The bill was vetoed by two Republican Presidents—Coolidge and Hoover.

The demand for electric power out West, however, was far greater than private power companies could fulfill. So in 1928,

Hoover signed a Congressional bill authorizing the Hoover Dam (called at first Boulder Dam) at Las Vegas, Nevada. The dam was the first to be built by the government to do more than just irrigate arid land. Apart from irrigation and electric power, the Hoover Dam also provided flood control and the improvement of river navigation.

In 1928, Congress also passed a Flood Control Act providing for levee work on the lower Mississippi at a cost of $325 million. It was becoming apparent that the American people were determined to harness and control the key waterways of the nation in scientific ways that would both prevent devastation and spread the benefits of water power.

Senator George Norris, who had unsuccessfully tried to get two Republican Presidents to agree to government operation of Muscle Shoals, was finally successful when Democrat Franklin D. Roosevelt entered the White House in 1933. Soon after his election, F.D.R. visited the Tennessee Valley.

"Muscle Shoals," he declared afterward, "is more today than a mere opportunity for the Federal Government to do a kind turn for people in one small section of a couple of states. Muscle Shoals gives us the opportunity to accomplish a great purpose for the people of many states and, indeed, for the whole Union. Because there we have an opportunity of setting an example of planning, not just for ourselves but for the generations to come, tying in industry and agriculture and forestry and flood prevention, tying them all into a unified whole over a distance of a thousand miles so that we can afford better opportunities and better places for living for millions of yet unborn in the days to come."

Congress promptly passed the Tennessee Valley Authority Act of 1933—now generally known as TVA. This act set up a public corporation to develop the economic and social well-being of an area covering parts of seven states. For the first time in their lives, Americans living in rural areas of these regions were able to have electric lights and refrigerators and oil furnaces, operated at low rates. As one farmer jubilantly exclaimed, "We're in the twentieth century now!"

Before TVA, the per capita income of people who lived in this region was only 44 per cent of the national average. The use of cheap electric power raised that figure to 60 per cent by 1950. TVA also curbed floods, helped make year-round navigation on the Tennessee possible, supplied essential power to Atomic Energy Commission projects, and attracted many new industries to the region for its low-cost power. Significantly, TVA electric power costs less than half as much as the power supplied by private utilities elsewhere.

The private utilities are not happy about TVA, and have fought it bitterly since its inception. They point out that they pay heavy taxes to the government, and TVA does not, accounting for its ability to charge lower rates. They also condemned TVA as "socialism," and declared that it was unfair for all Americans to be taxed for TVA in order to benefit those living in seven states. But the Supreme Court upheld the right of the TVA to sell electricity as it wished.

"TVA is neither fish nor fowl," admitted Roosevelt with a jaunty grin, "but whatever it is, it will taste awfully good to the people of the Tennessee Valley."

It did. It still does.

Another vital F.D.R.-inspired piece of Congressional legislation that year was the Civilian Conservation Reforestation Relief Act. This was an attempt to kill two birds with one stone. Young men needed jobs desperately. There was a vast amount of work to be done in conservation. Congress put both needs together and started the CCC—Civilian Conservation Corps.

Their ranks and accomplishments were vastly enlarged in 1935 with the passage of the Emergency Relief Appropriation

Act authorizing the expenditure of $5 billion to provide "work relief . . . by providing useful projects" under the Works Progress Administration, known as the WPA. In the eight years this program lasted, fully 8,500,000 Americans had found employment in useful public works. Republican critics bitterly attacked WPA projects as "boondoggling"—meaning wasteful and inefficient work which accomplished little—but they could not get around the fact that it gave employment to vast numbers when employment was desperately needed.

The Soil Conservation Act of 1936 helped farmers, at the same time it prodded them toward soil-conserving practices, by paying them to take some crop acreage out of production. This act by Congress laid the groundwork for the Soil Bank program in operation today, designed to reduce farm production without reducing farm income.

Another important step forward in the development of our natural resources was in the direction of international cooperation—the St. Lawrence Seaway Act of 1954. President Dwight D. Eisenhower called Congress's passage of this bill "a historic victory." It represented the final agreement, after twenty years of argument, to work together with Canada in the construction of a seaway to connect the water systems of both nations.

if the United States had not agreed to pass this bill, Canada was ready to build the St. Lawrence Seaway herself. But the bill was vital to American interests. The seaway now links Midwestern ports with Europe through the Atlantic. It also guarantees the United States an emergency supply of iron ore from Labrador, essential because our principal source of high-grade iron ore in Minnesota's Mesabi Range is starting to run out.

As America grew more prosperous in the postwar years, with more and more cars, buses, and trucks crowding the highways, the annual death rate in auto accidents began to climb. In 1955 more than 38,000 Americans lost their lives on the highways—

far more in that one year than were lost in the American Revolution, War of 1812, Mexican War, and Spanish-American War combined.

Congress passed the Highway Act of 1956 to develop a United States network of national highways that would let Americans cross their country with speed and safety. It was a $32 billion project, the most gigantic federal undertaking in road-building in the century and a half since Jackson vetoed the Maysville Bill.

"The concrete poured to form these roadways," observed President Eisenhower, "would build eight Hoover Dams or six sidewalks to the moon."

Congress seems well on the way now toward voting to build "six sidewalks" to the moon. In 1966 President Lyndon Johnson proposed that a Secretary of Transportation be added to the Cabinet, signifying that the future developing of modern and safe paths of travel—on earth and in space—will be a government responsibility.

And when aerospace explorations of the moon and neighboring planets make some of their natural resources available to the nation, Congress will unquestionably pass new legislation directing their development and use for the good of all.

7

Laws for the Worker

Steelworkers in the mills of the "Little Steel" companies were fighting mad. In their struggle to organize a union, they had been fought by espionage, strikebreaking, blacklists, and private armies of thugs wearing company badges. Leading the war against them was Tom Girdler, tough president of Republic Steel.

Now angry crowds of striking workers and their wives were milling outside the Republic plant in south Chicago on the afternoon of May 27, 1935. They threw rocks, sticks, and stones at cars that sped scabs—nonunion workers—through picket lines in front of the company gate. When the excitement died down, many of the strikers began walking toward their parked cars to leave for home.

Suddenly an armored truck shot out from the main entrance. Uniformed company guards, heavily armed, leaped out into the middle of the street. They began firing upon the dispersing crowds. People scattered in panic, screaming. The guards chased them, firing as they ran. Men and women were clubbed down in the gutter. A group of children were caught in the hail of gunfire as they were returning from school.

To add to the terror and confusion, company guards hurled tear-gas bombs into the crowds. More were fired from the roof of a Republic Steel building.

The attack led to a Senate subcommittee investigation by Senator Robert M. La Follette. One eyewitness, Darrell C. Smith, testified, "It was almost beyond description, Senator. It was just about the bloodiest scene of enactment in America."

He recalled, "I saw women struck with those iron bars just as mercilessly as though they were men. I saw a group of school children across the street running around in a panic, scared, crying at the top of their lungs because they were frightened out of their wits by this tear-gas shooting that was going on all around them. These guards were rushing around the people, and beating the people to the brick pavement, and then beating them after they were down."

Pending in Congress at this time was the Wagner Labor Relations Act, making it compulsory for all employers to recognize, then sit down and bargain with unions representing their workers. This law was precisely what the steelworkers had been trying to achieve in their bloody struggle against Little Steel.

Thirty-eight days after the brutal attack of Republic Steel company guards on men, women, and children in south Chicago, an outraged Congress passed the Wagner Act.

Although the Wagner Act made possible the tremendous growth of the CIO and industrial unionization in America, Little Steel continued to defy the act for another two years. On Memorial Day, 1937, Republic Steel company guards once more fired into crowds of striking workers, their wives and children, killing ten and wounding forty.

The earliest trade unions in America go back to Washington's time. These were actually guilds of skilled workers: carpenters, cabinetmakers, weavers, hatters, and others. To fight these combinations, employers frequently used the courts to brand the guilds as "illegal conspiracies . . . guilty of a combination to raise wages." By the 1850's, however, local guilds began to join hands in national combinations for protection.

The first effective national labor organization was the Knights of Labor, which began as a secret order and grew swiftly in major importance during the 1880's. Composed of all types of workers, the Knights supported several major strikes, which they won, and increased in size to a 700,000 membership. But by 1890 this labor organization was already declining because of bad leadership and dissatisfaction among skilled workers.

The appearance of the Knights on the national scene symbolized a change in the nation's economic picture. Until 1880 the United States was largely a nation of independent farmers, artisans, and shopkeepers. But the coming of the Industrial Revolution converted Americans into a nation of wage earners dependent upon the sale of their labor to big companies or corporations.

Workers of this new economy found themselves faced with new threats of every sort—jobs going to those willing to work for starvation wages, mill shutdowns, industrial accidents, constant pressure to produce more even as piecework rates were cut. The government and the courts seemed indifferent to their hardships.

So workers began to depend more and more on themselves. They organized the unorganized into unions, and used the strike, the boycott, and the picket line to force employers to establish a fair wage scale, shorter hours, and humane working conditions. Out of the ashes of the Knights of Labor they built a new and stronger national union—the American Federation of Labor.

Led by a shrewd cigar maker named Samuel Gompers, the AFL continued to regard the government as its enemy, the ally of big business. Presidents and state governors used troops against strikers. Laws were passed to curb strikes, boycotts, and other economic weapons used by the AFL. Courts granted injunctions to employers to help them break strikes. In effect, the forces of law were used on the side of powerful capitalists against a growing labor movement.

In 1896, when popular resentment against the big corporations resulted in the passage of the Sherman Antitrust Act, many courts came to the rescue of big business by using the Act against labor unions as "illegal combinations of workers." The AFL began to feel increasingly that it would have to enter politics to influence legislation and enforcement on the side of the working people, rather than of capital.

The AFL helped to elect President Woodrow Wilson and a Democratic Congress in 1912. Its first reward was the Clayton Antitrust Act of 1914, which specifically exempted labor unions from the antitrust laws, forbade the use of court injunctions to break strikes, and declared that strikes, boycotts, and peaceful picketing were not violations of federal law.

Another breakthrough for labor came the following year with the La Follette Seamen's Act, which prescribed minimum wages, food, and quarters required for seamen sailing on ships under American registry. There was sympathetic public support in 1915 for merchant seamen because of the sinking of American freighters by German warships.

Another labor landmark came out of Congress the following year—the Adamson Act of 1916, establishing an eight-hour day for railroad workers, with time and a half for over-time. When Congress passed the bill and President Wilson announced that he would sign it promptly, the railroad brotherhoods called off a national strike set for the next day, Labor Day.

Thus the Wilson administration helped bring about a changing view of the labor situation in America—namely, that the law should protect labor unions and encourage the spread of collective bargaining, to help equalize the struggle against the all-powerful, wealthy giant corporations.

With the return of Republican administrations following World War I, however, this sympathetic view of labor unions was sharply curbed. All through the booming 1920s, when jobs were plentiful, membership in the AFL fell off, and millions of workers remained unorganized. Congress maintained the status quo on behalf of big business, not passing significant legislation that might rock the boat of Coolidge-Hoover prosperity.

But after the stock market crash of 1929, followed by an ever-deepening depression, hundreds of thousands of workers joined the ranks of the jobless every month. The government seemed paralyzed by indecision, either unwilling or unable to pass new laws that would pull the nation out of its terrible plunge into a depression that eventually left as many as eleven million Americans jobless—one in every four.

William Green, who succeeded Gompers as head of the AFL, declared gloomily, "Men are afraid, workingmen are filled with fear." The growing roar of protest swept the Republicans out of office in 1932, and ushered in the "New Deal" administration of President Franklin D. Roosevelt.

Hoover, trying to appease labor during the presidential election year of 1932, signed the first prolabor union bill of the Republican decade—the Norris-La Guardia Act. The new law made it illegal for an employer to interfere with his workers' attempts to organize a union; stopped the practice of getting court injunctions against strikes; and forbade "yellow-dog" contracts—contracts with workers which compelled them to agree that they would not join unions.

The Norris-La Guardia Act was another victory for labor, but it did not save Hoover from defeat in November.

In the first year of Roosevelt's administration, Congress passed a powerful prolabor law—the National Industrial Recovery Act of 1933, which attempted to spread work, shorten hours, raise wages, end child labor, and guarantee the rights of collective bargaining. Two years later, however, the Supreme Court heard a test case and ruled the NIRA unconstitutional.

The setback was only temporary. What followed in 1935 was the Magna Carta of American labor—the Wagner National Labor Relations Act, which inspired cries of anguish from the business community. This act put the American government firmly in labor's corner, and guaranteed the success of the labor movement in organizing the nation's unorganized workers.

The Wagner Act prohibited five types of unfair labor practices by employers—interfering with workers' rights to bargain collectively; dominating or in any way influencing labor unions; discriminating against union members in either hiring or firing, or for exercising his rights under the Wagner Act; refusing to bargain collectively with the union agents chosen by a majority of the workers. Under the Wagner Act, a company could not set up a company union in order to avoid having its workers join an outside union.

The act also set up a National Labor Relations Board (NLRB) to investigate all complaints of unfair labor practices, to issue restraining orders to the guilty companies, and to supervise elections when necessary to determine the true choice of representatives by the employees of a company.

The Wagner Act, with subsequent amendments, is still the law of the land today, and can almost be considered labor's own "Bill of Rights." To a great extent it equalized the power between workers on the one hand and corporations on the other. It has been criticized, and continues to be, for having in some cases made a few unions *too* powerful.

By opening the way to a great labor organizing drive in the United States, the Wagner Act inadvertently led to a split in the labor movement. William Green, head of the AFL, wanted organizing to continue along the lines of craft unions—all carpenters in one big union, all auto mechanics in another, and so on.

But John L. Lewis, head of the powerful United Mine Workers led a strong group of unions who wanted vertical unionization—that is, organizing all employees of a big corporation into *one single union,* regardless of their type of work. They argued that it would be easier to strike and shut down a company if all its workers were represented by the same union.

The result of all this was that a group of unions broke away and called themselves the Congress of Industrial Organizations, or CIO, and they were led by Lewis. The CIO grew strong and powerful by following its ideas for unionizing the auto, steel, and other basic industries, protected by the Wagner Act.

In 1936 Congress gave further support to union objectives by passing the Walsh-Healey (Public Contracts) Act. This law required corporations having contracts with the federal government to operate on a forty-hour work maximum, paying at least minimum wages, and employing no child labor.

By 1938, when the shock had worn off the business community, Congress introduced these same provisions for *all* companies whose products were sold across state borders. The Black-Connery Fair Labor Standards Act, F.D.R. explained, was intended to put "a ceiling over hours and a floor under wages." The act has been amended at regular intervals ever since, to raise the minimum wage according to the cost of living.

John L. Lewis, who was even fiercer in fighting for the rights of his coal miners than he was as head of the CIO, made a tactical mistake in 1943, when the nation was at war. Defying both F.D.R. and the War Labor Board, he took the coal miners out on strike and won his demands for them. Congress was outraged by his indifference to America's war effort.

The result was the Smith-Connally War Labor Dispute Act, which provided penalties for anyone who promoted a strike once the government seized a plant or industry and made a thirty-day "cooling-off" period mandatory. Roosevelt, fearful that this act might cripple all the gains labor had made during ten years under the New Deal, vetoed the bill. Congress passed the act over his veto. It marked a turning of the tide.

After the war, when the Republicans won the Congressional elections of 1946, they controlled the 80th Congress that constantly fought with Democratic President Harry S. Truman. Under the leadership of Senator Robert Taft, Congress passed the Taft-Hartley Act of 1947, over Truman's veto. This important bill has been highly controversial.

Essentially, Taft-Hartley amended the Wagner Act by defining and prohibiting "unfair practices of labor organizations." Forbidden were the closed shop (every worker required to join the union recognized by his company); featherbedding (unions requiring more men to be hired for jobs than were really needed); excessive union initiation fees; secondary strikes (boycott of a company's customers).

Taft-Hartley further required a sixty-day notice of intention to strike; affidavits by union officials to certify that they were not members of the Communist Party; an eighty-day postponement of any strike that might endanger public safety or health; and the filing of a union's financial reports with the Secretary of Labor.

A coalition of Republicans and Southern antilabor Democrats kept Congress from repealing the Taft-Hartley Act, which the AFL and CIO both called a "union-busting law," and John L. Lewis denounced as "a slave law unpalatable to free-born citizens." The act did tend to make it more difficult for the AFL and CIO, which reunited in 1955, to organize workers in the South. But Taft-Hartley has essentially been more in the nature of a thorn in the side of labor, rather than a major obstacle to the growth of the union movement.

On the plus side, the act has also helped to check some malpractices by corrupt unions and union officials, and to that extent protected the workers in those unions.

It has also received quiet but effective support from many liberal Americans who once opposed it bitterly, because of the stubborn "public be damned" position taken by many powerful unions in calling strikes against the public interest. Strikes which particularly angered the public during 1966, and lost the union movement a great deal of popular sympathy they once enjoyed, were those in the transportation industries—strikes that grounded the flights of many national airlines, and halted the subways of New York, creating serious hardships for millions of Americans who had nothing to do with the conflicts between labor and management that penalized them.

8

Laws Regulating Business

Americans in the last quarter of the nineteenth century were seething with indignation at the high-handed extortion policies of corporation and railroad monopolies. The Supreme Court had said that they could not be curbed by state law because their activities took them across state lines. This was the age of the great "robber barons" who built up industrial fortunes—Carnegie, Morgan, Vanderbilt, Gould, Rockefeller.

"It's unjust!" the farmer of that day protested bitterly to his representatives in Congress. "I have no way of getting my products to market except on the one railroad serving our region. The railroad sets the rates as high as it can without bankrupting me. I have to pay whatever it asks or go out of business!"

"Its unjust!" the Eastern worker growled to his congressman. "Food and everything else we buy is so expensive because the big corporations have set up trusts, so that every company charges the same high price. And when the railroads take their share of the grab, the prices of things to the consumer go up even further to line *their* pockets!"

"It's unjust!" the small oilman protested to his representatives in Washington. "The Marietta and Cincinnati Railroad charges me thirty-five cents a barrel to haul my crude oil, but they only charge Standard Oil ten cents a barrel for the exact same haul.

Not only that, but they give Standard Oil the extra twenty-five cents a barrel they charge *me,* as a rebate!"

For a while the mounting tide of protest produced a great deal of state legislation regulating railroad rates, but the Supreme Court held all these laws unconstitutional when it handed down the decision in *Illinois v. Wabash, St. Louis and Pacific Railroad* in 1886, on the ground that only Congress had the power to regulate interstate traffic.

Many labor, farm and small business groups now began to demand that Congress, which had been reluctant to put any controls on big business, take action with a strong new federal law. This led to the passage in 1887 of the Interstate Commerce Act, which forbade railroads to grant special rates or rebates, to charge more for a short haul than a long haul, or discriminate in any way among its customers. Only fair and reasonable rates were to be charged, and an Interstate Commerce Commission was appointed to supervise rates and investigate complaints.

With this major legislation, the American people in effect said to their big corporations, "The price of free enterprise is responsibility to the public by those who operate it. If in the future you do not live up to that responsibility, we will see to it that the Government *forces* you to."

But the powerful railroads were not willing to give up without a fight, and kept the Interstate Commerce Act largely ineffective by constant court battles. It was not until Theodore Roosevelt became President in 1905, sworn to curb the trusts and monopolies, that the Interstate Commerce Commission was given the power to enforce the Act.

The Hepburn Act of 1906 gave the ICC real authority, letting them set maximum rates, extending their jurisdiction to storage facilities, express companies and pipelines, and forcing railroads to break up their trusts with steamship lines and coal companies. The Mann-Elkins Act of 1910 let the ICC suspend any railroad's rate increase while studying its "reasonableness"—or lack of it. It also extended the ICC's jurisdiction to telephone, telegraph, and cable rates.

The railroads were the first to feel the impact of the public's anger against the trusts. Three years after passing the Interstate Commerce Act, Congress passed one of its most famous pieces of legislation—the Sherman Antitrust Act of 1890. This bill outlawed all contracts, combinations, or conspiracies in restraint of trade, and all monopolies. It was aimed directly at some of the leading offenders—Standard Oil, the whisky and sugar trusts. The act was not intended to cripple the giant corporations, only curb them and increase competition, so that the public benefited from lower prices.

There were many weaknesses in the act, however, and big business was not slow to take advantage of them. The wording was vague, and the trusts used every loophole to avoid compliance. Punishments were treated with contempt—the maximum was a $5,000 fine and a year in jail, with the jail term used only against labor unionists and racketeers, not against businessmen.

One of the first test cases was the government's suit against the American Sugar Refining Company, which controlled 98 per cent of the refined sugar capacity in the United States. Although it was a clear monopoly, the company's lawyers argued that the act did not apply to it because it was not engaged in "interstate commerce." Their reasoning: the manufacturing of sugar was not commerce, but *prior to commerce*! The corporation-minded Supreme Court of that day awarded them the verdict.

After fifteen years of thumbing their noses at the act, the big corporations knew a day of reckoning was at hand with the election of "trust-buster" Teddy Roosevelt. "As far as the antitrust laws go," he vowed, "they will be enforced, and when suit is undertaken it will not be compromised except on the basis that the Government wins."

He directed the Department of Justice to wage an all-out campaign of enforcement. During his administrations there were twenty-five indictments against the trusts. Railroad tycoons Harriman and Morgan were ordered to break up a Mississippi railroad combination. The beef trust was forbidden to engage in practices restraining competition. Standard Oil was broken up into several separate companies. The tobacco trust was shattered.

Despite these victories, the trusts continue to operate in various disguised ways, and to reorganize in different kinds of combinations. Rockefeller grunted contemptuously when the Standard Oil edict was handed down: "Humph! The combination is here to stay. Individualism has gone, never to return." The fact that there were more trusts, rather than fewer, at the end of Roosevelt's terms in office suggested that Rockefeller was right.

On the other hand, it was labor, rather than big business, that was punished by antitrust legislation. In 1902 the Danbury hatters of Connecticut went out on strike, and organized a boycott of the Loewe Hat Company products. The company sued the union and its members, charging them with being guilty of restraint of trade in violation of the Sherman Antitrust Act. The business-minded Supreme Court found the union and membership guilty, and in a 1908 decision (*Loewe v. Lawlor*) ordered them to pay the stunning sum of $300,000 in damages.

Public wrath grew at the trusts and the administrations that seemed unwilling to take effective steps to curb them. When Theodore Roosevelt broke with President Taft, splitting the Republican Party to form his rival Progressive Party, he said accusingly, "I stand for the square deal . . . property shall be the servant and not the master of the commonwealth."

Woodrow Wilson was swept into office on a wave of antitrust sentiment. One of his first pieces of legislation, enacted by

Congress in 1914, was the Federal Trade Commission Act. It set up the FTC as an industrial policeman, watching business methods to eliminate unfair methods of competition that might result in monopoly. Anyone—individual, small businessman, or business rival—could complain to the FTC and request an investigation of business malpractice.

One of the most important functions of the FTC today is that it also polices advertising, to protect consumers from false and misleading statements by manufacturers. In this watchdog capacity, it prevents the public from being sold dangerous drugs, useless nostrums, misrepresented shoddy goods.

The Wilson Congress also passed the Clayton Antitrust Act of 1914, which was designed to plug holes in the Sherman Antitrust Act. "The Congress has sought," Wilson said, "in the Trade Commission bill and in the Clayton bill, to make men in a small way of business as free to succeed as men in a big way, and to kill monopoly in the seed."

The Clayton Act spelled out specifically a list of illegal acts by big business, and exempted labor unions from any antitrust legislation. It contained two new and impressive prohibitions. Company directors were forbidden to be directors of, or hold stock in, a rival company. Corporation officers were also made *personally* liable for violations.

This provision of the Clayton Act had startling repercussions almost half a century later, when forty-five executives of all the nation's leading electric companies were found guilty of conspiring to rig prices, resulting in overcharges on government contracts of up to 900 per cent. The shocked judge sent seven of the $100,000-a-year executives to prison, fined forty-four a total of $137,500, and gave twenty-one suspended five-year sentences.

Critics of antitrust legislation persistently maintained that the government was wrong in penalizing bigness and monopoly in business, maintaining that only the giant corporations and combines could operate so efficiently that the end result would be cheaper cost of production and lower prices to the consumer. When the depression began, Gerard Swope, head of General Electric, felt that big business could lead the way out by cooperating to establish conditions that would lead to economic stability.

He drew up an eight-point "Swope Plan" that called for industries to work together in trade associations, stabilizing industry prices and controlling distribution. When the plan was submitted to the White House, no less a conservative than President Herbert Hoover was shocked by its implications for the Sherman and Clayton Antitrust Acts.

"There is no stabilization of prices without price fixing and control of distribution," he wrote to his Attorney General. "This feature at once becomes the organization of gigantic trusts such as never have been dreamed of in the history of the world. This is the creation of a series of complete monopolies over the American people. It means the repeal of the entire Sherman and Clayton Acts, and all other restrictions on combinations and monopoly. . . . It is the most gigantic proposal of monopoly ever made in this country."

Hoover's objections killed the Swope Plan.

The Sherman and Clayton Acts continue to be the bulwark of protection against the tyranny of industrial monopoly for the American consumer. In 1966, eight of the nation's largest steel companies were indicted for price-fixing that had caused price jumps on washing machines, refrigerators, automobiles, and other everyday American necessities.

At one time railroad tycoon Cornelius Vanderbilt had been able to sneer to a reporter, "The public be damned!"

Most tycoons today have too healthy a respect for the enforcement of the Sherman and Clayton Acts to risk indictment, stiff fines, and even prison sentences by defying the acts out of greed for excessive profits.

On the other hand, the government is indicating that it no longer opposes business mergers and combines on the grounds of bigness alone, where the end result seems to be for the public good. In late April, 1966, for example, the ICC gave permission for the New York Central and Pennsylvania railroads to merge, on condition that they take over and operate the bankrupt New Haven Railroad, and that no employees of any of the three railroads lose their jobs as a result of the merger.

This unusual and important ruling of the ICC may indicate the beginning of a new government policy to encourage larger combinations of public carriers for greater efficiency and public service, under government regulation.

9

Health, Education and Welfare Laws

The terrible phenomenon was happening all over Germany and England. Five thousand horrified German couples and a thousand British couples were stunned when their babies were born with shocking deformities—without limbs or with stubby, seal-like flippers. European doctors were mystified. American doctors wondered fearfully how soon this strange new epidemic would spread to the United States.

At the Food and Drug Administration in Washington, a woman doctor settled into her new job of passing on the application of drug companies for licenses to market new drugs. She was Canadian-born Dr. Frances Kelsey, who had both practiced medicine and taught pharmacology. One of the first applications she studied was from a Cincinnati drug company that wanted to produce a sleeping pill containing the drug thalidomide under the brand name of Kevadon. The company asked for quick FDA approval, but Dr. Kelsey had her doubts about the drug.

Reports of its tests on animals and humans indicated that it somehow failed to put animals to sleep. Why? She asked the company to make more tests. Meanwhile, searching through European reports, she found one from England stating that it could cause a tingling neuritis in some patients. Her knowledge of pharmacology led her to suspect this symptom as a possible danger to pregnancy. She kept delaying approval of Kevadon for over a year, while the company fumed impatiently.

Then at the end of November, 1961, German medical investigators suddenly announced that they had found the cause of the terrible epidemic of deformed babies. The mothers had taken blue sleeping pills . . . thalidomide!

Dr. Kelsey promptly rejected the Kevadon application, and the FDA flashed warnings around the country to all doctors who may have given the pills out experimentally.

For her alertness in protecting thousands of American parents from the tragedy of thalidomide, Dr. Kelsey was presented with the President's Award for Distinguished Civilian Service. And Congress passed a new bill called the Drug Industry Act of 1962, which gave the FDA more time to study drug applications, and tightened up the requirements for drug companies to prove a new drug's safety and effectiveness.

When the new law passed the House of Representatives, its members stood up and applauded wildly—a rare demonstration in Congress of the 1960's.

"It's not often," one congressman explained to a reporter, "that we can do something like this directly for the people!"

Today's youth in America grow up feeling that the federal government has always been a benevolent, protecting force looking out for the welfare of its people. But the truth is that as late as the beginning of this century, Washington largely avoided passing such laws. The American tradition was "Do for yourself," and *"Caveat emptor*—let the buyer beware."

Poverty was considered not quite respectable, even an indication of low moral character. Why should the middleclass and affluent Congress pass laws to favor the "most worthless" elements of the population? Influential voices of the nineteenth century urged both the federal and state governments to leave help for the poor up to the mercies of private charity.

Economist Francis Wayland condemned any welfare laws to help the needy, however grudging, because they implied that "the rich are under obligation to the poor." Sociologist Herbert Spencer also opposed public relief because it prevented nature from wiping out unemployed "good-for-nothings."

Life was hard for working-class minority groups in the big cities. They depended for help largely on political ward bosses to keep from starving or freezing in bad times. They paid for this help with their votes, and the politicians they elected then grew fat on the city graft. No one in such times dreamed of suggesting that Washington should be helping *all* citizens with health, education and welfare laws.

The first feeble federal legislation in this direction was passed in 1798. Because of hostilities between France and England, with America caught in the middle, Americans grew anxious about our sea commerce. Shipping out on American vessels grew ever more dangerous. To encourage and support our seamen, Congress passed the Marine Hospital Services Act, providing them with prepaid medical and hospital care.

The importance of the Marine Hospital Service is that it gradually grew into the Public Health Service, which is now part of the Department of Health, Education and Welfare.

Early in the twentieth century voices began to be heard expressing outrage against the way big business was cheating, gouging, and exploiting American consumers. Newspaper and book exposes, written by angry reporters called "muckrakers," brought about a growing demand for government legislation.

Chief among the muckrakers who brought this pressure to bear were Dr. Harvey W. Wiley, chief chemist of the Department of Agriculture, who exposed dangerous drugs and patent medicines, and Upton Sinclair, whose exposure of working conditions in the Chicago stockyards in his book *The Jungle* provoked nationwide revulsion against the meat packers.

At first President Theodore Roosevelt praised the crusaders for the public service they were performing. But then Wall Street and the trusts angrily applied pressure behind the scenes. In March, 1906, Roosevelt suddenly reversed himself and denounced "muckraking" writers and magazines like *McClure's.*

But New York's Governor Charles Evans Hughes, later Chief Justice of the Supreme Court, defended them.

"When there is muck to be raked, it must be raked," he declared, "and the public must know of it, that it may mete out justice. . . . Publicity is a great purifier because it sets in motion the forces of public opinion, and in this country public opinion controls the courses of the nation."

On June 30, 1906, Congress passed the Pure Food and Drug Act, prohibiting the mislabeling or adulteration of food and drugs sold in interstate commerce. On the same day it also passed the Meat Inspection Act, providing for the inspection by the Department of Agriculture of the conditions of slaughter and packaging of meat intended for sale across state borders. Both laws were a giant step forward in wiping out the worst abuses of the food and drug manufacturers.

They also clearly spelled out a new direction of government policy—federal control of business to the extent necessary to protect the public. President Woodrow Wilson underlined that new policy in his 1913 Inaugural Address.

"The first duty of law is to keep sound the society it serves," he declared. "Sanitary laws, pure-food laws, and laws determining conditions of labor which individuals are powerless to determine for themselves, are intimate parts of the very business of justice and legal efficiency."

Today's Food and Drug Administration, now part of the Department of Health, Education and Welfare, enforces the famous edicts of 1906 so that modern American families can depend upon the purity, safety, and honest labeling of the food and drugs they buy in the nation's stores.

The muckrakers also brought to light a scandalous condition involving the employment of child workers. In the latter half of the nineteenth century, almost two million children between the ages of ten and fifteen were employed in factories and mines, working long hours for starvation wages under miserable and dangerous working conditions. One investigator found six- and seven-year-old children canning vegetables in a factory at two o'clock in the morning.

John Spargo, a muckraker whose book *The Bitter Cry of the Children* (1906) appalled the nation, described a scene he saw in the Pennsylvania and West Virginia coal mining region:

"Crouched over the chutes, the boys sit hour after hour, picking out the pieces of slate and other refuse from the coal as it rushes past the washers. . . . The coal is hard and accidents to the hands, such as cut, broken or crushed fingers, are common among the boys. Sometimes there is a worse accident; a terrified shriek is heard, and a boy is mangled and torn in the machinery or disappears in the chute to be picked out later, smothered and dead. Clouds of dust fill the breakers and are inhaled by the boys, laying the foundation for asthma and miners' consumption."

They were ten and twelve years old, working for fifty cents a day, and some of them had never been inside a schoolroom.

Some states had child labor laws on their books, but they were completely inadequate and unenforced—a smokescreen to keep local reformers quiet. In the new climate of Woodrow Wilson's campaign for progressive reforms, some states hastily began passing child labor laws with teeth in them. Massachusetts adopted a minimum wage law for children and women, the first such legislation in the country.

On April 9, 1912, Congress passed an act creating the Children's Bureau under the Department of Labor. Staffed primarily by women, it was charged to investigate and report "upon all matters pertaining to the welfare of children and child life among all classes of people." Now under the Department of Health, Education and Welfare, the bureau works together with each state's own children's bureau to be sure that children everywhere are protected, and that those who require special help of any kind get it.

In 1916 Congress went further with a law forbidding the interstate shipment of any product made with child labor, the Keating-Owen Child Labor Act. The Supreme Court, however, declared this act unconstitutional two years later. So the use of child labor, while subject to the scrutiny of the Children's Bureau, continued through the 1920's.

Congress moved further in this direction in 1921 by passing the Sheppard-Towner Act, providing federal aid to the states for maternity and child-welfare services. Under this act today public health nurses visit the homes of impoverished, expectant mothers, children benefit from school health programs, and services are provided for crippled, blind, retarded, and neglected children.

Strict regulation of child labor did not come until the Great Depression of the 1930's, when one out of four Americans was out of a job. It was this crisis, rather than the plight of child workers, which led to the passage of new legislation raising the age required for employment. The more children who were forbidden as cheap labor to employers, the more jobs would become available to out-of-work adults.

The New Deal passed a series of bills designed to curtail child labor, but ran into trouble when the Supreme Court declared some of them unconstitutional. In 1938, finally, Congress passed the Fair Labor Standards Act. It banned from interstate commerce all goods manufactured in industries employing children under sixteen, or under eighteen in industries judged hazardous by the Children's Bureau. Three exceptions were made.

Younger children could work in agriculture when they did not have to attend school. Also exempted were children employed by their own parents in enterprises other than mining or manufacturing. Exempted, too, were fourteen- and fifteen-year-olds, except for mining or manufacturing, when their jobs did not interfere with their well-being, health or schooling.

Many critics feel that this act, and most of the states' own child labor laws, are still too weak and full of loopholes. But thanks to Congress, the terrible exploitation of children described by John Spargo is today no longer legally possible.

The Depression brought about a great change in attitude in the United States. With so many millions of Americans reduced to desperate circumstances, the feeling that there was something personally shameful in poverty vanished. And the states soon exhausted their own welfare resources. Everyone looked to the federal government for help.

In 1933 Congress responded by passing the Federal Emergency Relief Act, setting up the Federal Emergency Relief Administration to match funds with state and local governments in distributing aid to the jobless. This was the first time in American history that the government had acknowledged its responsibility to come to the rescue of those citizens who were unable to find work to support themselves and their families.

President Roosevelt stressed the importance of social justice and said, "Change is the order of the day."

But the most significant and far-reaching legislation of the New Deal was the Social Security Act of 1935, strengthened and improved by a 1939 amendment. It was tailored to reflect F.D.R.'s bold belief: "A government that could not care for its old and sick, that could not provide work for the strong, that fed its young into the hopper of industry, and that let the black shadow of insecurity rest on every home, was not a government that could endure or should endure."

The Social Security Act provided a federal program of old-age benefits, based on the workers' earnings before the age of sixty-five, to be paid out of deductions from their wages matched by a payroll tax on employers. Grants were set up for the states so that workers out of a job could collect unemployment insurance for a set period of time. Grants to the states were also made for aid to needy dependent children, maternal and child welfare services, medical work among crippled children, welfare services for the aged and the blind.

"Security from the cradle to the grave," F.D.R. called it. "Socialism!" screamed its critics, largely Republicans. But the American public felt that Social Security was a valuable and reassuring floor of support beneath the average family, and since the act was passed no administration has ever dared to suggest repealing or curbing the Social Security Act.

Another bold change in the American direction was the New Deal's conviction that the government had an obligation to fight slums, and provide inexpensive, decent homes for those citizens who could not otherwise leave the slums.

Congress passed the Wagner-Steagall Act in 1937, setting up the U.S. Housing Authority as part of the Department of the Interior, to make long-term, low-interest loans to state and municipal agencies for slum clearance and housing projects. Low-income families were given an annual subsidy to pay the difference between what they could afford and what the rent should be. Local authorities were required to eliminate one slum apartment for every new slum-clearance apartment built. The Housing Authority also undertook low-cost rural housing.

Slums are still with us, but vast numbers of former slum dwellers are now living in government housing projects. In 1950

Congress passed another Housing Act, authorizing the use of as much as $1.5 billion in slum clearance and the erection of low-cost housing.

Perhaps no single administration in American history has enacted as much legislation as that of President Lyndon B. Johnson, or so many bills of major significance. The Congress under Johnson has also emphasized new laws in the field of health, education and welfare, as part of Johnson's attempt to lift all Americans into his "Great Society."

For Johnson's "fight on poverty" Congress passed the Economic Opportunity Act of 1964, setting up a Job Corps to educate, train, and support out-of-school youth to help them get jobs. Another 1964 law extended and expanded the National Defense Education Act, with all kinds of loans and grants to help more students go on to college and graduate education.

A new Housing Act of 1964 authorized more than a billion dollars to help homeowners repair their homes and to keep from losing them by foreclosure, as well as to make funds available for housing of the elderly and handicapped.

President Johnson made a flying tour of the chronically poverty-stricken Appalachia area including parts of Ohio, Pennsylvania, West Virginia, Virginia, Kentucky, Maryland, Tennessee, North Carolina, Georgia, and Alabama. Shocked at what he saw, he urged Congress to pass a $250,000,000 program to relieve poverty and develop economic resources in this region containing fifteen million Americans.

"I strongly urge the Congress," he declared, "to attach to this bill the urgency and the need that is so plainly written on the faces of Appalachian citizens. They are looking to you and to me for help so they can help themselves."

In 1965 Congress passed the Appalachia Act.

Another historic bill was the 1965 Elementary and Secondary Education Act, the first proposal for aid to elementary and secondary schools ever to win congressional approval, although bills had been introduced for this purpose since 1881. This aid-to-education law provides $1.3 billion for five different kinds of help to low-income school districts.

The 1965 Congress also took a vital step forward to protect the health of the nation, and especially of the young, by acting on the Surgeon General's report linking lung cancer and other diseases to cigarette smoking. The new law requires all cigarette packs and cartons to carry the warning, "Caution: cigarette smoking may be hazardous to your health."

Another enormous change in American life came about through the 1965 Social Security Law providing for Medicare—health insurance for Americans sixty-five years or older, to relieve the elderly of the crushing burden of doctor and hospital bills when they are most apt to incur them and least able to afford them.

New legislation of almost equal significance to the Pure Food and Drug Act of 1906 is pending to stop the shocking annual total of 50,000 deaths a year in automobile accidents. Thanks largely to the exposures of Ralph Nader, a modern "muckraker" attacking the automobile industry for turning out "death traps on wheels," Congress has set up federal standards of car safety which all manufacturers will be compelled to follow.

America's health, education and welfare laws have taken the nation a long way from the days when it was considered that the federal government had no right or obligation to help and protect the individual American citizen and his family.

10
Laws for the Farmer

"You're a fool to stay, John," his neighbor said grimly, stopping an old jalopy loaded with possessions and family to say good-by before migrating to California. "This mean old dust bowl's gonna bury everybody who don't get out—farmers, stock, and houses clear up to the chimney!"

John White, whose farm lay in the far west of Oklahoma, stared around him with hard, stubborn eyes. The dust storms of the early thirties had left all his crops parched and withered. His horses were dying in the fields, their lungs clogged with dust. It was necessary for him to herd his cattle into a corner of the barnyard and shoot them, one by one.

Poor farming practices and overgrazing had made the dust bowl—50 million acres including parts of Oklahoma, Texas, New Mexico, Colorado, and Kansas—especially vulnerable to the terrible drought that struck in 1930. Lacking sufficient vegetative cover, the soil was stripped away by howling dust storms that turned day into night.

The high hot winds piled sand and earth against houses, fences, and barns in dunes four to ten feet high. Crop failure and loss of topsoil ruined thousands of farmers. One out of every three Oklahoma farmers gave up and became "Okies"—surrendering their farms to the dust as they migrated hopefully to the farmlands of California.

John White was one of the stubborn ones who held on, despite his dismay at watching much of Oklahoma blowing away from under his feet. He loved the land too much to leave it, and he doubted that California would prove a paradise for the dust bowl refugees. So he stayed on hopefully, praying for better luck next year, somehow managing to keep his family alive.

Congress came to his relief at the end of 1930 with a Drought Relief Act, authorizing the appropriation of $45 million for farmers like John White. So, though the going was hard and bitter, he survived the depression years and stayed on the land where he had been born and raised.

Thirty years later John White owned a 4,700-acre farm of high productivity, a fine ten-room house, five trucks, 400 head of cattle, and was doing so well that he even owned a small private plane. To a large extent his good fortune could be traced in the laws which Congress began to pass to help the American farmer keep the nation in food.

Congress today recognizes that the welfare of the farmer is vital to the whole country. Because the conditions of his livelihood are peculiarly different from those of other Americans, Congress has tried to make sure that he is not penalized for it. Laws have helped insure him against the wheel of fortune when he has bad luck in weather or market prices.

Toward the end of the nineteenth century the farmer began to get indignant at his low share of American prosperity. He worked hard every day from "kin to can't"—from the time he could see to the time he couldn't—with few of the conveniences or advantages enjoyed by his fellow citizens in towns and cities. The mechanization of fanning forced him to buy expensive machinery and implements. The interest charged him on bank loans was so steep that he was plunged into debt.

By 1890 more than 90,000 farms in Illinois and 100,000 in Nebraska were heavily mortgaged. The farmer felt helpless, outraged. He had been too busy, too isolated, to elect farmers to Congress to represent his interests. As a result Washington legislation largely favored the interests of manufacturers, bankers and railroad men, while neglecting the farmers.

Chief exception was the year 1862, when a wartime Congress passed a number of farm bills. The Homestead Act granted free farms of 180 acres each to those who agreed to occupy and improve them for five years. The Morrill Act sought to raise farm standards of living by providing grants of public lands to establish agricultural colleges as centers of farm training and research. These colleges have been largely influential in developing improved agricultural methods, and in educating the American farmer in their use.

In 1862 Congress also established a new Department of Agriculture to help the farmer increase productivity, halt soil erosion, and protect him from market price fluctuations. It did not achieve Cabinet status, however, until 1889 when discontent among farmers began to alarm Eastern industrial interests.

To express their grievances, farmers began to join in granges, then farmers' alliances, finally in the Populist Party.

"Wall Street owns the country," accused Populist leader Mary Lease. "It is no longer a government of the people, by the people, for the people, but a government of Wall Street, by Wall Street, and for Wall Street. Our laws are the output of a system that clothes rascals in robes and honesty in rags!"

Agriculture fought industry in the election of 1896, when the Populists supported Democratic candidate William Jennings Bryan against Republican William McKinley. The Republican victory brought a decline of the Populist movement and a renewed government apathy toward problems of the farmer.

Campaigning in 1912, Woodrow Wilson accused, "No Republican administration, no Republican Congress, has attempted to serve the farmer as he ought to be served in the matter of credits. It is practically impossible for the farmer to borrow money on the kind of securities ordinarily demanded at the banks. . . . He can't be mortgaging his farm every time he needs a little money!"

When Wilson was elected, a Democratic Congress swiftly indicated its concern for the farmers' needs. In 1914 the Smith-Lever Act arranged for county agents, working under the Department of Agriculture and state agricultural colleges, to bring the latest and best farming knowledge and techniques directly into farm communities, working with farmers.

Then in 1916 Congress passed the Federal Farm Loan Act, creating twelve Federal Land Banks to provide long-term, low interest loans to farmers. Signing it, Wilson said, "The farmers, it seems to me, have occupied hitherto a singular position of disadvantage. . . While they have sustained our life, they did not, in the same degree with some others, share in the benefits of that life. . . . One cannot but feel that this is delayed justice to them."

The booming twenties were a prosperous time for most Americans, but many farmers did not share the boom. Wheat, corn, and cotton farmers were in trouble because foreign competition, recovered from World War I, was underselling them overseas. Women were wearing less and less cotton. And with many farms mechanized, farm output flooded the American market, sending agricultural prices into the cellar. Many farmers went broke and left the land for the bustling cities.

Realizing that the government had to help, President Herbert Hoover asked Congress to pass the Agricultural Marketing Act of 1929. This act created a Federal Farm Board to encourage the marketing of farm products through cooperatives. The Board helped to buy up and hold commodity surpluses until there was a scarcity, in that way shoring up farm prices.

The act was a failure because farmers simply produced even more surpluses, and the board ran out of funds after tying up half a billion dollars in stored commodities.

The Depression made the farmer's plight desperate. Sheriffs began foreclosing on unpaid mortgages. Furious farmers began to band together to take the law into their own hands, driving sheriffs and deputies off the farms they tried to take over on behalf of creditors.

President Franklin D. Roosevelt moved quickly to help the farmers stave off disaster. Eight days after his inauguration in 1933 his Democratic Congress passed what has ever since been the cornerstone of the American farm program—the Agricultural Adjustment Act. It authorized the payment of cash subsidies to farmers who curtailed the acreage of surplus crops and the number of surplus livestock. The funds were obtained by taxing processors of farm commodities, such as cotton ginners, meat packers, and flour millers.

The purpose of the act, F.D.R. explained, was to keep farm product supply and demand in balance, keeping prices at a level that would give farmers the purchasing power of city workers. When the act was passed, however, crops for the year had been planted and livestock had been bred. So Secretary of Agriculture Henry Wallace ordered the plowing up of above-quota cotton and the slaughter of above-quota pigs.

There was a violent outcry against this order as an absurdity. "We are bribing farmers to sabotage food in a hungry world!" one critic protested. "The New Deal is a senseless system—an economy of waste and nonproduction!"

"To hear them talk," Wallace replied sarcastically, "you would have thought that pigs are raised for pets."

Farmers in danger of losing their farms by mortgage fore-closure were saved in June, 1934, by the Frazier-Lemke Farm Bankruptcy Act. If they couldn't meet their mortgage payments, they were given a five-year grace period, during which time they simply had to pay rent to their creditors. When the five-year time span was declared unconstitutional, it was revised to three years, and this time the law held.

Another historic innovation for the farmer came in 1935 with the Rural Electrification Administration, established at first by executive order, then passed as a bill by Congress. Its purpose was to bring electricity to millions of farms that had been neglected by private power companies. In 1930 only 10 per cent of farms had electricity. By 1945, almost half did. The REA meant not only modern comforts for the farmer and his family, but also power for improved farming methods.

Although things were looking up for most farmers under the New Deal, the poorest of them—sharecroppers and tenant farm-ers who did not own their own land—comprised 42 per cent of the farm population. In 1935 a new government agency, the Resettlement Administration, tried to take poor farm families off worn-out land and resettle them on good farms of their own.

In 1937 Congress passed the Bankhead-Jones Farm Tenant Act setting up the Farm Security Administration. The FSA was empowered to make long-term, low-interest loans (forty-year loans at 3 per cent) to tenant farmers, sharecroppers, and farm laborers whose applications were approved by local committees, for the purpose of letting them buy their own farms. By 1950 this Act had reduced the number of tenant farmers by 27 per cent. After World War II, the Farm Security Administration was replaced by the Farmers Home Administration, which also helped GI's buy farms.

Meanwhile, how was the highly individualistic American farmer reacting to government quotas, controls, and subsidies under the Agricultural Adjustment Act? In late 1935 a referendum was held in sixteen corn-and-hog states to let farmers decide whether they wanted the AAA to continue. By a vote of 6 to 1 they enthusiastically urged its continuance.

But early the next year the Supreme Court decided that the act was unconstitutional on the ground that its tax on processors was not levied for the general welfare but to control agricultural products not necessarily in interstate commerce. In 1937, however, death and retirement brought changes to the conservative Supreme Court, so that Congress was encouraged in 1938 to pass a new Agricultural Adjustment Act.

This bill restored the policy of supporting agricultural prices, and of providing for production controls when necessary. The processor tax was eliminated. Payments were made to farmers who shifted production from soil-depleting to soil-building crops. Commodity loans were granted on surplus crops. Farmers were guaranteed price supports on wheat, corn, cotton, rice, peanuts, and tobacco at 90 per cent of "parity"—that is, of farmers' purchasing power during 1909–1914, when they had enjoyed a period of high prosperity.

This act, which the Supreme Court held to be constitutional, made farm income by 1939 double what it had been in 1932. Its policies have essentially been those of subsequent Agricultural Acts passed since that time.

The 1949 Agricultural Act reaffirmed the provisions of the AAA, and is still the backbone of today's price supports to the farmer. The 1958 Agricultural Act set up a Soil Bank program, under which farmers who agreed to take acreage out of production received 50 per cent of their average income from that acreage, and also part of the cost of conservation practices.

The Agricultural Act of 1962 was enacted only after prolonged controversy. Senator Everett Dirkson, Republican minority leader, charged that "it drives the farmer toward regimentation!" The act provides subsidies for farmers for taking land out of production and either putting it in the Soil Bank or utilizing it for water, forest wildlife, or recreation resources, It also authorizes loans to state and local agencies to carry out plans for such land utilization.

There is widespread discontent with the agricultural laws. Many farmers welcome the financial security Congress has given them, but chafe at government restraints and red tape. Housewives upset by the high cost of food resent the subsidies that help keep prices high. Small businessmen argue that the government doesn't guarantee *their* prices. Taxpayers are irate over the billions of dollars paid out of the Treasury to farmers as subsidies. Worst of all, the farmers who benefit *most* are those wealthy enough to own huge acreage.

The basis of our difficulty, ironically, is that American farming has become so efficient that one modern farmer using modern machinery can produce the food that it once took a hundred American farmers using simple tools to supply. We simply have millions more farmers today than we need. As long as they choose to stay on the land, they will continue to form a farm bloc of votes that Congress cannot ignore in legislation.

11

Laws Regulating Morality

One day in the spring of 1900, Benner Tucker, urbane bartender of the elegant Senate Bar of Topeka, Kansas, did not notice the tall woman in a navy blue cape and black poke bonnet as she entered his saloon. Suddenly he heard sounds of chopping. Wheeling around, he stared in amazement as Mrs. Carry Nation calmly hacked away at his carved and polished solid cherrywood bar with a bright shining hatchet.

"Hey! What in blazes do you think you're doing!"

"The work of the Lord!" she shouted. "Hallelujah!"

Tucker grabbed the revolver he kept behind the bar. Leveling it at her, he advanced slowly. "Give me that hatchet!"

She finished chopping a chunk out of the bar, then turned and swung the hatchet at his head. "Maker of drunkards and widows!" she screamed. "Destroyer of men's souls!"

He ducked the whirling weapon, snatched it from her hand and fired two shots into the ornate ceiling.

"Police! Police!" He ran out the rear door.

Carry Nation produced a spare hatchet from under her cape. She slammed it against the giant mirror behind the bar. It cracked and fell in huge shards. Sweeping the hammer along the shelves, she sent rows of liquor bottles crashing to the floor.

"The arm of God smiteth!" she cried. Then she lifted the cash register and hurled it to the floor in an explosion of metal, bells and silver. Chopping the tubing which carried beer from tanks to faucets, she aimed the cut tubes at the walls and ceilings and drenched the saloon in beer.

Then the police came and led her away.

"All the police in the world will not stop Christian Temperance Union!" she screamed. "Other women with hatchets will destroy the saloons of America, and save American men from a drunkard's fate!"

And all over America, for the first dozen years of the 20th Century, women did pick up hatchets and invade saloons to smash them, following the example of Carry Nation. Their hatchets were a powerful force that led to the only Congress ever made to legislate individual morality—Prohibition, the "noble experiment" that failed.

The early Americans, who often had harsh laws about personal morals, never thought of making drinking illegal. Everyone drank whisky, wine, beer, or cider, from ministers to two-year-old babies. If anyone had tried to crusade against "the demon rum" in the colonies, he would have been kicked out of the community as either demented or some kind of radical.

In the 1700's, for example, the ordination of a New England minister was the signal for a giant drinking celebration. At the ordination of Rev. Edwin Jackson at Woburn, the joyful congregation polished off almost seven barrels of cider, twenty-five gallons of wine, two gallons of brandy, and four gallons of rum.

Before the Revolution, offices in Boston, New York, Philadelphia, and Baltimore closed at 11 a.m. so that everyone could get to the taverns for "Leven o'clock Bitters." Every home fireplace had an iron poker called a loggerhead, which was heated and used to stir a rum-and-beer drink called a flip.

Not until 1826, in Boston, did the first forces organize in a crusade against intemperance, under the banner of the American Temperance Society. They campaigned for pledges of teetotalism because (1) alcohol injured the mind and body; (2) it impoverished men and their families; (3) it led to vice and crime; (4) it created a tax burden to provide institutions for those whose lives it wrecked; (5) it made workers inefficient; (6) it made Americans unfit for church, social, and civic life.

As the nation became prosperous, intoxication grew increasingly rampant. Even a distinguished Frenchman visiting America in 1831, Alexis de Tocqueville, was appalled by the extent of drunkenness he found in Boston.

"They live very well in Boston," said the aristocrat, to whom wine was a civilized accessory to meals. "They have but a single fault, which is that of drinking too much."

Former President John Adams, residing in Boston, thought so, too. He strove to get the Court of Sessions to reduce the number of licensed taverns, but failed.

"You might as well preach to the Indians against rum," he snorted in disgust, "as to our own people."

Temperance societies, however, kept fighting for state laws banning the manufacture and sale of liquors. Their growing pressure forced such laws through in Maine, Vermont, Minnesota, Michigan, Rhode Island, Massachusetts, Connecticut, Indiana, Delaware, Pennsylvania, New York, and New Hampshire, between 1851 and 1855, a period of intense antiliquor agitation.

The temperance drive received powerful support from two eminent Americans, P. T. Barnum, the great showman, and Horace Greeley, the fighting journalist. Barnum produced a famous melodrama, *The Drunkard,* dramatizing the horrors of drink, and urging the audience to sign temperance pledges at the box office on the way out. Like Greeley, Barnum often lectured against the evils of drink, and had a stooge planted in the audience to ask him, "How does alcohol affect us, Mr. Barnum—externally or internally?"

"E-ternally!" Barnum would reply to great applause.

Greeley enthusiastically endorsed *The Drunkard,* and carried on a lifelong anti-alcohol crusade in the famous New York *Tribune* he edited. A teetotaler who blamed drink for ruining his father's life, Greeley drank required toasts at banquets by filling his glass with a red rose to simulate wine.

Despite the temperance societies, Barnum, Greeley, and state laws, Americans refused to stop drinking. Liquor sales were so profitable that the United States, in 1862, finally sought to raise money for the Civil War by taxing them. Congress passed the first internal revenue act, charging every liquor establishment a fee and putting a manufacturers' tax on beer, ale, and spirits.

Following the war, saloons multiplied all over America. By 1900, New York, Buffalo, and San Francisco had a saloon for every 200 citizens. The saloon was regarded as "the poor man's club," offering fraternization as well as alcoholic escape from worries and responsibilities. Defying all local and state ordinances, saloon owners evaded fees and taxes, through the protection of corrupt politicians they bribed.

There was widespread intoxication on Saturday night, which was payday. A mill hand could get exhilarated for fifty cents, dead drunk for a dollar. Around midnight men streaming home from the saloons would screech, sing, quarrel, and fight. Those who refused to visit the saloons, or lived in dry states, would often get drunk on patent medicines, of which the principal ingredient was pure alcohol.

The temperance forces girded their loins for battle. A Prohibition Party was formed. An Anti-Saloon League joined the W.C.T.U. in all kinds of crusades against drinking. They supported the State of Kansas when an action was brought to declare the state's prohibition act illegal because it violated the 14th Amendment forbidding laws abridging the privileges of United States citizens. The Kansas Supreme Court decided that the state's prohibition act was simply a police regulation protecting public health and morals.

With that encouragement, Frances Willard of the W.C.T.U. led women into saloons, where they would fall to their knees, sing psalms, and pray. This unnerving tactic, which sent many an American male scurrying home, brought on Carry Nation's decision to invade the saloons with hatchets rather than psalms.

So successful were the tactics of the W.C.T.U. and the Anti-Saloon League that by the time World War I broke out, they had succeeded in banning the liquor traffic in more than half the states, and two out of three Americans were living under local or state laws which made it illegal for them to drink. Now the temperance forces joined for the supreme objective—a *national* law outlawing alcohol throughout America.

They did not receive much encouragement from Woodrow Wilson, both before and after he became President. As early as 1892 he had written, "The state ought not to supervise private morals." He never changed his mind. But in 1918, with the country at war, the temperance forces were winning congressmen to the view that if soldiers had to stay sober to fight properly, then defense workers ought to sacrifice the right to drink to stay healthy, efficient, and productive on the home front.

Wilson disagreed. "I have received delegations of working men," he declared, "who, apparently speaking with the utmost sincerity, have declared that they would regard it as a genuine hardship if they were deprived of their beer, for example. There is no arguing with feelings of that sort, and just because there is no arguing with them, there would be no way of handling them in this time of crisis."

But there was another subtle force at work which favored the pressure of the "drys" over the protests of the "wets." The enemy was German, and most of the big brewers and distillers were of German origin. The Anti-Saloon League stressed the number of loaves of bread that could be made from grain "wasted in a single day by the brewing of beer and distillation of spirits." Congressmen were asked whether they favored the liquor traffic which aided the enemy, or a Prohibition law which would help the American war effort.

Congress passed a wartime Prohibition act that turned the country dry in 1919. Flushed with victory, the drys decided to press ahead for *permanent* Prohibition, through an amendment to the Constitution. So in October, Congress passed the Volstead Act, prohibiting the manufacture, sale, or transportation of intoxicating liquors. Wilson angrily vetoed the bill, but it was passed again over his veto, and became the Eighteenth Amendment in 1920 when two-thirds of state legislatures ratified it.

"This law," confidently stated John F. Kramer, the first Prohibition commissioner, "will be obeyed in cities, large and small, and in villages, and where it is not obeyed, it will be enforced. . . . The law says that liquor to be used as a beverage must not be manufactured. We shall see that it is not manufactured. Nor sold, nor given away, nor hauled in anything on the surface of the earth or under the earth or in the air."

It was a highly inaccurate prophecy.

Many communities were angrily opposed to Prohibition. Bootleggers—those who carried on liquor traffic in violation of the law—had plenty of money with which to corrupt law enforcement agents. The 1920's saw the rise of the bootlegger, the hijacker, the racketeer and the gangster, as organized crime took over the supply and distribution of illegal liquor.

"Prohibition itself was a false issue," insisted presidential adviser Bernard Baruch. "We never did have Prohibition in this country; the law was on the books but was simply ignored. I once asked William Jennings Bryan why the Prohibition law did not punish the buyer as well as the seller. . . . The law as it stood was worse than useless. I couldn't see how any Dry could continue to favor a statute and support an Administration which had made such a farce out of law."

Liquor smugglers had 18,700 miles of American coastline on which to land supplies of liquor. Illicit stills were easily set up in the cellars of private homes everywhere. For $500 anyone could set up a commercial still producing 50 to 100 gallons of spirits a day, and get rich in a hurry. Speakeasies—illegal drinking places—sprang up everywhere as drinking became the "smart" thing to do. Most were gangster-controlled.

If drinking had been distressingly widespread before Prohibition, it became worse now. Millions of women, who had hitherto never been interested in drinking, now joined their husbands and boy friends in speakeasies and at cocktail parties. Violating the Volstead Act was considered a mark of sophistication.

The Republican administrations that followed Wilson—those of Harding, Coolidge, and Hoover—were marked by a flat refusal to admit that the Eighteenth Amendment was a dismal failure. But the bootleggers and rum-runners laughed and grew rich. Rum ships stayed safely twelve miles offshore and transferred their liquor cargoes by night to fast cabin cruisers, which were met on shore by graft-protected gangland trucks. The greater danger to them was not from the law, but from hijacking by other gangs.

The manufacture, importing, transportation, and sale of liquor became America's biggest business. Protected by bribed police and government officials, gangsters flourished. Al Capone, a Chicago gangster, quickly developed a crime empire based on alcohol which placed him above the law during the lawless 1920s. He and other Prohibition gangsters battled for supremacy on city streets, in broad daylight, with machine guns. Americans grew more and more dismayed at what Prohibition had done to corrupt law enforcement and respect for the law.

Baruch, who at first had supported Prohibition, admitted ruefully, "I have trouble believing that I advocated Prohibition. It was a blight which permeated our national life. I can only say, like the late Fiorello La Guardia (mayor of New York), 'When I make a mistake, it's a beaut!'"

The American people, appalled by what was going on, looked for a scapegoat. The wets accused the drys of playing into the hands of bolshevism by forcing an unenforceable law through Congress, causing a breakdown in law and order. The drys accused the wets of encouraging contempt for the law, thus fostering bolshevism.

By 1928 Prohibition was a major political issue. Governor Alfred Smith of New York City won the Democratic nomination for President as a wet. Herbert Hoover, who called Prohibition "a great social and economic experiment, noble in motive and far-reaching in purpose," was ostensibly a dry. But he promised a study of the problem by a government commission.

Hoover won the election, primarily because Americans voted for a continuation of Republican prosperity, and also because they had never yet elected a Catholic to the White House. Soon after election Hoover appointed the Wickersham Commission to study Prohibition enforcement. In January, 1931, the Commission admitted that there had been a definite breakdown in enforcement, and that the law was definitely distasteful to the American people who freely violated it. But the Commission cautiously recommended giving the law further trial.

Hoover's acceptance of the Wickersham Report made him extremely unpopular. At a baseball game he attended, he heard thousands of fans chant in unison, "We want beer! We want beer!" They didn't stop until he left the park, humiliated.

The dry era in American history came to an end on December 5, 1933, under President Roosevelt, after sixteen miserable years of failure. The legislatures of three-fourths of the states ratified the Twenty-first Amendment, which repealed the Eighteenth or Prohibition Amendment. Control of the liquor traffic returned to the states and there were only eight which continued to impose Prohibition under state law.

State Prohibition after 1933 proved no more successful than the federal variety. Writing thirteen years later, John Gunther reported in *Inside U.S.A.*, "'Dry' as the South may be in some spots, it is also the hardest-drinking region I have ever seen in the world, and the area with the worst drinking habits by far. Bars are not permitted in most cities; hence, people drink by the private bottle, and hypocrisy begets disorderly behavior. Never in Port Said, Shanghai or Marseilles have I seen the kind of drinking that goes on in Atlanta, Houston, or Memphis every Saturday night."

Some dry states, while pretending that they had abolished the liquor traffic, saw nothing inconsistent in collecting "a black market tax on illegal liquor." Will Rogers once wryly observed, "Mississippi will drink wet and vote dry—so long as any citizen can stagger to the polls." In 1966 *Newsweek* reported that the dry states of Mississippi and the Carolinas "boast some of the most prosperous bootleggers in the United States."

The miserable experience of the American people with Prohibition proved that Woodrow Wilson had been right when he warned, "The state ought not to supervise private morals."

Congress never tried it again.

12

Our Depression Laws

Unaware of danger, the President-elect of the United States, Franklin D. Roosevelt, was enjoying a sunny parade in an open car with Chicago's mayor, Anton J. Cermak. The two were in Miami; the date was February 15, 1933—seventeen days before F.D.R. was to be sworn in as America's thirty-second President.

Also in Miami on that day was a mentally ill bricklayer named Giuseppe Zangara. He had been having strange visions which foretold that he was destined to kill a "great ruler." Now, his gun loaded and checked, he waited with trembling anxiety for the car with F.D.R. to roll within his killing range.

He knew that he held within his hands the power to change the future destiny of a whole nation, just as thirty years later another assassin, Lee Harvey Oswald, was to stun the world by shooting and killing President John F. Kennedy.

Now the car with the President-elect drew close to Zangara's position. With a cry of jubilation he raised his gun and fired several shots. The crowd roared in horror as one of the two men in the car, struck by a bullet, writhed in agony. Zangara was seized and rushed off to prison.

His victim had not been F.D.R., but Mayor Cermak, who died of the bullet wounds. Public outrage against Zangara was so great that he was rushed to a speedy trial, with a swift verdict of guilty resulting in his execution only a month and a half after his crime. But because of his poor aim, Zangara had failed to change the course of American history.

Had he been successful in pursuit of his mad vision, there is no doubt that the Democratic administration of 1933–1936 would have been a vastly different one. The Vice-President, conservative old John Nance Garner of Texas, would have been inaugurated in Roosevelt's place. Instead of the now historic New Deal of the Roosevelt era, we might have had an administration not vastly different from Herbert Hoover's.

And many of America's greatest laws would never have been passed, with their major influence on our life today.

The Great Depression, which began in October, 1929, with the collapse of the stock market, kept snowballing through the last three years of the Hoover administration. By the end of 1932 there were fifteen million jobless Americans. Many tried to keep their families in food by selling apples on the street corners of the cities. Many begged, giving rise to the theme song of the 1930's "Brother, Can You Spare a Dime?"

Homeless men slept in subway stations, freight cars, tin shacks. Farmers could not meet mortgage payments and lost their homes. Savings were used up in staying alive during the crisis, and banks began closing their doors. Many Americans were kept from starving to death by bread lines and soup kitchens. In the Midwest, desperate farmers receiving only two cents a quart for their milk began dumping milk bound for market. Thousands of angry war veterans and their families joined the Bonus March on Washington in the summer of 1932, demanding that Congress pass a bill to give them an immediate bonus.

Obviously, something was very wrong with the American economic system. A group of engineers urged the nation to consider a new plan called "technocracy," which would turn

over economic control of the country to engineering techni-
cians—those who managed industry, rather than those who
owned it.

Hoover, who had vainly hoped that the depression would
correct itself, was forced to take some government action since
business was paralyzed by a lack of funds. He cautiously agreed
to try priming the economic pump from the top. In January,
1932, Congress passed the Reconstruction Finance Corporation
Act, setting up the RFC to lend $2 billion to banks, insurance
companies, railroads, savings and loan associations, and farm
credit organizations.

The depression only deepened. The Bonus Army descended
angrily on Washington, and F.D.R. was nominated as the Democratic candidate. "I pledge you, I pledge myself," he told the
country, "to a new deal for the American people."

Now shaken and worried, the Republican Congress hur-
riedly began passing emergency legislation to cope with the crisis. On July 21st an Emergency Relief and Construction Act was
passed, granting more than $2 billion in loans to states for relief
funds and public works. The following day Congress passed the
Federal Home Loan Bank Act, setting up a dozen FHL banks
to make loans to mortgage-lending institutions, to prevent foreclosures and encourage new building.

But the Hoover Congress was too late with too little. In
November the American people swept F.D.R. into office with a
crushing 7,000,000 plurality, and the House of Representatives
went Democratic 3 to 1. There was also a warning note sounded
to the capitalist system. The Socialists and Communists combined had rolled up over a million protest votes.

Roosevelt saw himself as a crusader with a mandate to (1)
remember "the forgotten man" and rescue him quickly; (2) save
the capitalist system from itself by correcting its abuses and mistakes, making it responsive to the needs of the people; (3) get a

dynamic program of recovery started that would lift the nation out of the depression and back to prosperity.

But even as he took office, ruin stared the nation in the face. On the very day of the inauguration, the banks of New York, Illinois, Massachusetts, New Jersey, and Pennsylvania closed, following closings in Michigan and Maryland a month earlier. America's economic system was on the verge of collapse.

Franklin Roosevelt brought a whole new approach to Washington. The Republican Presidents before him had acted on the advice of the nation's most important industrialists. F.D.R. summoned new advisers to Washington—university professors like Adolph A. Berle, Jr., Raymond Mosley and Rexford Guy Tugwell; financiers like Bernard Baruch; labor leaders like William Green and Sidney Ilillman. They became his "brain trust." He felt, as John Kennedy did after him, that university economists would have fresh, bold and intelligent ideas for steering the nation's course in new directions.

They became his architects for the New Deal which the famous 73rd Congress translated into legislative action. The laws they passed introduced many significant changes into our government and the American way of life. The New Deal broke with every previous administration, which had operated largely on the principle of laissez-faire—"the best government is the government that governs least." F.D.R. firmly established the principle that the government should and must be directly responsible for the employment, security and well-being of the people. His enraged critics cried, "Creeping socialism!"

The new 73rd Congress was called into special session only five clays after his inauguration, to pass into law a series of New Deal measures that F.D.R. considered urgent.

"Washington has never seen anything like those first three months of F.D.R.'s administration," observed Bernard Baruch, the famous adviser of Presidents. "A steady flow of ideas emanated from the White House, and were quickly translated into legislation during the famous Hundred Days."

In no other period of American history were so many important laws passed so quickly. A disciple and admirer of F.D.R., Lyndon B. Johnson, later sought to imitate the record of the New Deal with his own "Great Society" program.

On March 9, 1933, opening day of the special session, Congress passed the Emergency Banking Act giving the President control over banking transactions, forbidding the hoarding or export of gold, and enabling the President to reopen the banks he had closed by proclamation of a "bank holiday," as soon as examination proved them in sound condition.

Three weeks later the Civilian Conservation Reforestation Relief Act created the Civilian Conservation Corps, mentioned earlier. The CCC gave unemployed young men jobs on federal construction and conservation projects. Working outdoors in national parks, forests, and reclamation areas, they drained swamps, cleared trails, planted trees, fought soil erosion.

May of 1933 saw the passage of three other important laws described elsewhere—the Federal Emergency Relief Act, the Agricultural Adjustment Act, the Tennessee Valley Authority Act.

At the end of that month Congress moved to protect the investing public against the kind of fraudulent practices that had led to an orgy of Wall Street speculation and the stock market collapse. A Federal Securities Act provided for federal registration and supervision of all new stock issues.

Called the "Truth in Securities" Act, it changed the old doctrine of *caveat emptor* (let the buyer beware). The President warned that now the seller had better beware of stiff penalties for misrepresenting stock issues. The following year Congress tightened the rules against speculators still further by an act creating the Securities and Exchange Commission (SEC) to supervise the stock exchanges.

Early in June, F.D.R. took adviser Bernard Baruch for a drive in a car specially built so that the polio-crippled President could drive it himself. F.D.R. parked on a high ridge and pointed to a village in the valley below.

"There's a bank in that town," said the President, "and it holds the mortgages and notes of all those people living there. Now what I want to know, Bernie—are we going to get recovery by squeezing these people out through the wringer by natural processes, or are we going to help them? I don't think we can put them through the wringer."

On June 13th, Congress passed F.D.R.'s Home Owners Financing Act, which set up the Home Owners Loan Corporation—HOLC—to refinance home mortgages. The new law promptly stopped the alarming wave of foreclosures which, up to that time, had soared to over a thousand a day.

The HOLC saved four out of five homes on which it made loans, and at the same time kept many lending institutions from collapsing. About a million homeowners benefited from the HOLC's helping hand. Most were able to pay off HOLC loans and the low interest charges.

Three days after the birth of the HOLC, Congress passed the most sweeping law of the New Deal—the National Industrial Recovery Act (NIRA), affecting every phase of the economy. A National Recovery Administration (NRA) was set up under General Hugh Johnson to work out with employers and employees of each industry a "code" for that industry. The code sought to eliminate unfair competition, set minimum wages and maximum hours, abolish child labor and sweatshops, create additional jobs, protect labor's right to collective bargaining.

Cooperating stores and factories displayed signs with a Blue Eagle, insignia of the NRA, and the announcement, "We Do Our Part." Codes were worked out for over five hundred different industries. The NRA forced Southern textile mills to stop employing child labor, and raise their minimum wages to $12 a week. One mill owner had been paying 180 an hour, but pointed to an average wage of $15 a week. The NRA found that this was true—because he worked his employees 84 hours a week.

"Well, our people like it that way!" he insisted.

The codes were far from perfect, but they did give new jobs to about two million workers by shortening the average work week. They also curbed some unfair business practices, and cut down sharply on the use of child labor. The NRA also established a National Labor Board, with Senator Robert F. Wagner of New York, to enforce labor's right of collective bargaining.

The comprehensive National Industrial Recovery Act also set up the Public Works Administration (PWA), administered by Secretary of the Interior Harold L. Ickes. The PWA gave 30 to 40 per cent grants to local public works projects to stimulate them—roads, schools, sewer systems, water systems, slum clearance. It also undertook federal projects.

In June, 1933, Congress passed the last major legislation of the Hundred Days—the Glass-Steagall Banking Reform Act, discussed in Chapter 2, guaranteeing bank deposits and so ending bank failures as public confidence was restored.

F.D.R. emerged at the end of the Hundred Days as a national idol, the leader whose brilliant ideas and political skill had saved the nation from disaster. Never before had any President been able to direct such a flood of vital legislation through Congress so swiftly. Americans were delighted by the story of one congressional committee chairman who complained he couldn't get members to agree on a New Deal bill.

"Lock em up without lunch until they agree!" F.D.R. told him with a jaunty grin. They were locked up. They agreed.

Feeling his power, F.D.R. didn't wait for the next session of Congress to get another New Deal measure moving. On November 9, 1933, he issued an executive order establishing the

Civil Works Administration (CWA), with Harry L. Hopkins as administrator, to provide emergency jobs for 4,000,000 unemployed over the winter until the Public Works Administration could start enough projects to employ them.

When Congress reconvened in January, 1934, Roosevelt announced that the cost of the nation's recovery program would reach $10.5 billion by June, 1935. Outraged conservatives began grumbling against the New Deal, charging it with "spending its way out of the Depression, rather than working out of it." But most Americans were grateful that things were getting better.

When F.D.R. spoke to both houses of Congress in January, 1935, he told them he felt the time had come to "quit this business of relief," and get 3,500,000 employable relief recipients off welfare rolls and into jobs. On April 8th, Congress passed the Emergency Relief Appropriation Act, allocating $5 billion to provide employment on "useful projects" under a Works Progress Administration (WPA). Administrator of the WPA was Harry L. Hopkins.

This became one of the largest government agencies, creating work of every kind. It set men to building roads, bridges, dams, parks, and schools, and women to making clothing or teaching in schools. Actors were paid to put on shows of all kinds, including Shakespeare and plays dealing with problems of the depression era. Artists were set to work painting murals in post offices and county courthouses.

By December, 1935, almost three million workers were on WPA payrolls. Before the program ended in 1943, it had helped almost nine million to find temporary jobs. And although it was often accused of "boondoggling"—spending federal funds for useless projects—the WPA actually made a great contribution to the nation in conservation work, federal road and building construction, the erection of schools and parks, and in bringing cultural programs to millions of Americans who had never before been exposed to such intellectual stimulation.

Many of the nation's greatest literary, artistic and theatrical talents, incidentally, were kept from starving by the WPA, and used their job opportunities in this program to develop the abilities which later made them famous.

Although the New Deal had widespread popular support, it was bitterly criticized in the press, about 90 per cent of which was openly anti-Roosevelt. Far from saving the capitalist system, the press charged, F.D.R. was steadily eroding it and leading America down the path of socialism. The President, knowing he could not count on a fair press, spoke to the people directly over the heads of the newspaper publishers in a series of "fireside chats" that explained his New Deal as it unfolded.

But the worst attack on the New Deal came not from the fourth estate, but from an ultra-conservative Supreme Court. An angry Brooklyn poultry dealer named Schecter refused to obey the NRA code governing the quality of the chickens he sold and the wages he paid his employees. When the case reached the Supreme Court, they decided on May 27, 1935, that the NRA was unconstitutional because the retail poultry business was not interstate commerce, and that the government therefore had no right to pass laws regulating it. In January, 1936, the AAA was also declared to be unconstitutional.

Roosevelt was furious. He accused the Supreme Court of making "horse-and-buggy" interpretations of the Constitution because six of the "nine old men" were over seventy—too old, he insisted, to remain in office. He later put forth a plan to increase the number of justices, obviously in order to swing the balance in favor of New Deal legislation.

His "Court-packing bill," as his foes labeled it, was indignantly attacked as a step toward dictatorship, putting the Supreme Court under the thumb of the President. Congress balked, and the bill was defeated. Roosevelt gave up the fight when resignation and death removed some arch-conservatives from the Court, changing its attitude toward the New Deal.

The new Court ruled as constitutional the Social Security Act, the NLRB, the Frazier-Lemke Farm Bankruptcy Act as revised, the Fair Labor Standards Act, the second AAA Act.

The American people did not shed too many tears over the disappearance of the NRA. The crisis was over; six million jobless were back at work by the beginning of 1936. Besides, the NRA had been a clumsy, cumbersome program, with many abuses. Complaints began to increase that the New Deal was destroying private enterprise by interfering in business activity. Georgia Democrats appealed to their Governor Talmadge, who referred to F.D.R. scathingly as "that cripple in the White House," to lead the United States out of "New Deal Communism."

But the impact of the New Deal on the American way of life was permanent. Roosevelt had established the principle of a powerful Executive, dominating the Legislative. He brought about a "modern" Supreme Court willing to make liberal interpretations of the Constitution. He led the American people to expect swift legislation to help them in times of economic emergency. He put the rights of workers and farmers on a more equal basis with the rights of businessmen. He set the course of American legislation toward greater social justice.

All of the reform measures of the Great Society of the sixties were, in effect, extensions of F.D.R's New Deal.

"Some people say that all this recovery has just happened," Roosevelt said in a 1936 campaign address at Chicago. "But in a complicated modern world, recoveries from depression do not just happen. The years from 1929 to 1933, when we waited for recovery just to happen, prove the point. But in 1933 we did not wait. We acted. Behind the growing recovery of today is a story of deliberate government acceptance of responsibility to . . .

save the American system of private enterprise and economic democracy—a record un-equaled by any government in history." He went on to compare the New Deal to an emergency hospital that had operated on dying patients.

"Now most of the patients seem to be doing very nicely" he added wryly. "Some of them are even well enough to throw their crutches at the doctor!"

The argument still rages today between liberals and conservatives over whether Roosevelt saved American capitalism and the country, or whether he took the first major steps toward a welfare state, "with security from cradle to grave."

Bernard Baruch, who frequently criticized F.D.R. through the days of the New Deal, wrote this about him in 1938:

"Complain, as anyone may, about Roosevelt, he has at least awakened from its lethargy our consciousness of the need of those who are generally termed 'the underprivileged.' If we do not go to sleep again and will do the right thing, everything will be all right. But no change in tax laws or any other laws will do us any good unless the great masses of people feel that they have been justly dealt with."

13

Laws for Soldiers
and Scholars

The trouble began when New York City's Sunday papers came out with long lists of names of New Yorkers drawn out of a lottery device—draftees for the Union Army. Many of those drafted were Irish-American mechanics and laborers, almost all of them Democrats bitterly opposed to "the Republicans' war." They were further embittered by a provision of the new draft law that favored the rich by exempting them if they hired a substitute, or paid the government $300 to hire one.

On July 11, 1863, government marshals who were turning the wheel of the draft lottery at the enrollment office at 46th Street and Third Avenue became uneasily aware that about a thousand sullen workers had gathered in a mob outside.

Suddenly a pistol shot was fired into the office, followed by an electrifying crash as stones came hurtling through windows. The mob burst into the office, smashed the lottery wheel, drove out the deputy marshals, and set fire to the office. The whole block was soon ablaze.

The rioters fought off police and surged through the city armed with clubs, paving stones and guns. They were joined by thousands of other draft protesters who came pouring out of factories and shipyards. Some carried signs: "The poor man's blood for the rich man's money."

"No draft!" they roared. "Kill the naygurs!"

Other mobs surged through other neighborhoods, giving New York the appearance of a city in revolution. Policemen and soldiers were attacked and clubbed to death. Negroes unfortunate enough to be on the streets were seized and hanged on trees and lampposts. Homes everywhere were put to the torch, filling the streets with flame and smoke. Huge gangs attacked the New York *Tribune* building, threatening to hang Horace Greeley for his support of Lincoln and the Civil War.

The riots, the worst in the history of any American city, continued for three days. Four hundred people were killed. Troops had to be ordered north from Gettysburg's battlefields before order could be restored.

The New York uprising was the price paid for the unpopular Conscription Act passed by Congress on March 3, 1863. Were the New York rioters correct in protesting that this act was undemocratic, favoring the rich over the poor? During the Civil War, 255,000 men were drafted. Of this number, 204,000 were substitutes, paid for by those who could afford to avoid serving.

More than a century later, Americans still found themselves hotly disputing the justice of the draft law, as the United States found itself embroiled in an unpleasant war seven thousand miles away in Vietnam.

There is good reason to consider laws for soldiers and scholars as one interrelated unit. Most soldiers are youths fresh out of school. In the America of today, military service is deferred so that those young men who want to, and are qualified, can go on to higher education. Finally, it has become a government policy to provide educational opportunities for those of its youth who have performed military service.

Significantly, almost right after the Civil War, Congress passed a bill in March, 1867, setting up a U.S. Department of Education. Congress made no attempt at national educational legislation, however, until another war threatened in 1917. Then in February it passed the Smith-Hughes Act, creating a Federal Board of Vocational Education to work toward this goal in cooperation with the states.

Right after America declared war on Germany, President Wilson asked Congress to draft troops. "The principle of the selective draft," he said, "has at its heart this idea: that there is a universal obligation to serve." But Congress was not eager to take this step to prosecute the war.

"There's little difference between a conscript and a convict," snorted one congressman, voicing the views of many. "Military service ought to be voluntary. Millions of immigrants came to this country just to escape conscription in Europe!"

Many congressmen were unhappy about offending special groups of voters back home—pacifists, Socialists, Irish-Americans, German-Americans, the anti-British. Southern congressmen were warned by their constituents of the dangers of giving Southern Negroes training with weapons.

But Wilson's appeals to the nation's patriotic sentiment stirred up a fervor that forced Congress to pass the Selective Service Act of 1917, based on the principle of universal conscription. All young men between the ages of twenty-one and thirty were compelled to register with their local draft boards, subject to military call. The age limits were later made eighteen to forty-five.

The draft was administered in democratic fashion by boards made up of civilians from the draftees' own communities. In the first month more than ten million men were registered. When a test case was brought against the Selective Service Act, the Supreme Court upheld it as constitutional.

But there were many protesting voices. In a speech to the Socialist Party convention at Canton, Ohio, on July 16, 1918, Socialist leader Eugene V. Debs declared, "You need to know that you are fit for something better than slavery and cannon fodder!" Arrested for this speech and tried under the Espionage and Sedition Act of 1918, he was given a ten-year jail sentence.

In the atmosphere of war hysteria that prevailed between 1917 and 1919, three Americans were hanged, 64 tarred and feathered, 55 kidnapped and whipped, and 1,100 thrown forcibly out of town, for speaking out against the draft or the war.

The end of World War I brought a return to civilian status of four million soldiers and sailors. On June 4, 1920, Congress passed the Army Reorganization Act, calling for a peacetime army of only 298,000. In October of that year veterans staged a big parade in New York City demanding that Congress vote them a war bonus. Many veterans were angered by the number of civilians who had prospered at home with war wages and profits, while they had fought a war for beggarly pay.

Congressmen grew nervous. Some thought of Shay's Rebellion, when angry veterans of the American Revolution staged violent riots all through Massachusetts. The courts had been issuing judgments against them for debts largely incurred because they had served so long in the Army. The government had given them nothing after the war to cushion the shock of readjustment to civilian life. Their explosive protests had narrowly missed growing into a full-scale revolution.

Congress hastily passed a bonus bill in 1922, but President Harding vetoed it. Congressmen tried to allay veterans' wrath by pointing to the Veterans Bureau Act they had passed in August, 1921, setting up the Bureau to handle insurance claims and payments, provide hospitalization for the wounded, and to provide vocational training for the handicapped.

But the roof fell in when a scandal broke in February, 1924, as Charles R. Forbes, who had been put in charge of the Veterans Bureau for two years by President Harding, was indicted for defrauding the government of $250 million dollars in corrupt contracts and shocking waste. He went to jail for two years for such frauds as buying $70,000 worth of floor cleaner, enough to last a hundred years, at 98¢ a gallon for cans not worth 4¢ a gallon.

Two months after the uproar this scandal provoked among veterans—"millions for graft, but not a penny for bonuses!"—Congress speedily enacted a new Soldiers' Bonus Bill, and passed it over Coolidge's veto. The Treasury was authorized to issue to veterans twenty-year paid-up certificates, against which they might borrow money from the government at 6 per cent interest. In 1931 the veterans demanded that they be paid the full amount of the certificates.

Congress, however, passed the Bonus Loan Bill, giving them cash loans up to 50 per cent of the certificate value. The following year veterans staged their famous Bonus March on Washington to demand passage of the Patman Bonus Bill, which would pay them the other 50 per cent. Under the pressure of 11,000 veterans camped in Washington, the House passed the bill, but it was rejected by the Senate.

Then President Hoover ordered the Bonus Army driven out of Washington by federal troops led by General Douglas MacArthur.

In 1940, with the Battle of Britain raging and a defeated France occupied by Germany, President Roosevelt felt that the preparedness of the United States demanded a new draft. In September, Congress passed the Burke-Wadsworth Selective Training and Service Act, the first peacetime draft in American history. It required the registration of all men between the ages of twenty-one and thirty-five, subject to a call-up for a year of military training. More than sixteen million men registered in October.

Thirteen days after the Japanese attack on Pearl Harbor, Congress replaced this law with a more all-embracing Draft Act, requiring registration of all men between eighteen and sixty-five, with liability for military service for all between twenty and forty-five. In November, 1943, Congress passed an amendment calling to the colors youths of eighteen and nineteen, after Roosevelt insisted that this was necessary for victory. By 1945 more than eleven million Americans were under arms.

When the suspense of D-Day was followed by General Eisenhower's successful invasion of German-held Europe, a jubilant and grateful Congress passed the Servicemen's Readjustment Act, more popularly known as the GI Bill of Rights. It provided for up to one year of unemployment pay at $20 a week for World War II veterans who failed to find jobs, as well as financial aid to self-employed veterans who needed it.

The government also guaranteed up to half of a $2,000 loan for ex-GIs who wanted to buy a home or farm, or start a business. The GI Bill also sought to provide war veterans with the education they had missed while in the armed services by letting them choose a college or vocational training school, paying $500 a year for tuition and books, plus at least $50 a month for subsistence.

The educational provision of the GI Bill was enormously popular, and after the war veterans crowded onto the campuses of the nation's colleges and universities. Often bringing wives and children with them, they introduced a new and more serious note to higher education which left a lasting impact. Many were from poorer homes, and without the aid of the GI Bill would have been unable to go to college. It was the GI Bill, more than any single factor in American life, that changed college from the privilege of a few to the goal of the many.

Out of that widespread college training, too, came hundreds of thousands of doctors, dentists, lawyers, engineers, scientists, and business executives who in the next twenty years helped raise the American standard of living to its highest level in the history of the nation.

When price controls were ended after the war, prices of building materials shot up so fast that the building of desperately needed homes was badly hampered. In May, 1946, Congress passed the Veterans' Emergency Housing Act, appropriating $250 million to convert army barracks, wartime housing, and defense worker trailers into temporary homes for veterans and their families. Many ex-GI's lived in these homes which were erected near the universities they were attending.

That year Congress beat more swords into pens by passing the Fulbright Act which provided that proceeds from the sale of surplus war materials to Allied countries should be used for educational fellowships allowing Americans to study and teach abroad, and foreigners to study and teach in the United States.

When the Selective Service Act ended on March 31, 1947, President Harry S. Truman urged Congress to pass a new draft law requiring compulsory military training for eighteen-year-olds. He felt that the cold war required a strengthening of American armed forces, which had largely been demobilized after the war.

"President Washington," Truman argued, "instituted the first military policy of the United States when he recommended a universal draft as a guarantee of basic minimum military protection for the Republic against aggressors. Washington's policy was not implemented until 1917, when President Wilson authorized the first compulsory draft. During the nation's other great crisis in the 1860's, the lack of a firm military policy resulted in

disgraceful draft riots and mob action, and in the corrupt practice of selling draft exemptions to individuals who could raise
the required sum."

But Congress, dreading the unpopularity of a peacetime
draft law, refused to consider one until the spring of 1948 after
the crisis of the Berlin blockade and the airlift. The Selective
Service Act of 1948 was bitterly opposed by many senators, but
became law on June 24th. It required young men from nineteen
to twenty-five to register, subject to call for twenty-one months
of military service. Any eighteen-year-old enlisting for one year
was exempted.

With atomic energy and scientific advances rapidly changing
the nature of the world we live in, as well as concepts of defense,
Congress passed a bill in 1950 to establish the National Science
Foundation to support scientific progress by subsidizing basic
research and education in the sciences. Emphasis was placed
on strong assistance to science teachers, students, and advanced
scholars. NSF grants have been responsible for new discoveries
and advances in the fields of aerospace, Antarctica, earth crust
and oceanographic studies, and in the new science of weather
modification.

The new importance of developing the best scientific brains
possible was made to seem more urgent by the space and mis-
sile race between the United States and the U.S.S.R. It became
more apparent to the American people that the best interests
of defense lay in keeping young scientists at their books, rather
than in siphoning off their talents and time in military service.
So in March, 1951, a system of draft deferment for college students was authorized on a basis of their scores in special tests.

In June, Congress extended the Selective Service Act and
lowered the induction age to eighteen and a half, adopting the
principle of universal military training as American peacetime
policy. This act has remained in effect ever since, modified

to require two years of active service, of which the first four months must be spent at American training centers. Deferred or exempt are ministers, divinity students, fathers, scientists, engineers, teachers, defense workers, family hardship cases, college students in the upper strata of their class, religious conscientious objectors, and those judged physically, mentally, or morally unqualified for military service.

With the Korean War raging in 1953, Congress voted in July for a new GI Bill extending the same benefits to Korean veterans as those given World War II veterans. A dozen years later Vietnam War veterans were given the same privileges.

With the hundreds of thousands crowding into college every year, educational experts warned President Eisenhower that only a crash program could develop all the teachers America would need by 1970. So at the President's urging, Congress passed the National Defense Education Act of 1958. The tag of "National Defense" was used to persuade economy-minded but patriotic congressmen to allocate $800 million for what was essentially federal aid to education.

The act called for a four-year program of loans to students who were preparing to follow teaching careers; grants to states for testing programs to locate gifted high school students; aid to schools needing special science, math and language teaching equipment; graduate fellowships for prospective teachers; grants for setting up special foreign language centers. To add a "defense" flavor, Congress stipulated that no one could borrow any NDE money unless he first signed a loyalty oath.

On principle, many educational institutions refused to support the student-loan program because of this McCarthy-like stipulation. President Eisenhower agreed that it was "rather deplorable." The requirement of a non-Communist affidavit was finally dropped by Congress when it voted a two-year extension to the act. Among those relieved to see this unnecessary note of red-white-and-blue hysteria removed from the bill was President John F. Kennedy, who said he was "glad to approve" its repeal.

A brand-new idea in legislation was introduced in 1961 under President Kennedy's New Frontier program. Scholar and soldier were blended to produce a new kind of army—the Peace Corps, composed of idealistic young volunteers dedicated to going overseas to live with the people of underdeveloped countries as technical helpers.

"It will not be easy," Kennedy warned. "None of the men and women will be paid a salary. They will live at the same level as the citizens of the country which they are sent to, doing the same work, eating the same food, speaking the same language. We are going to put particular emphasis on those men and women who have skills in teaching, agriculture and in health. I am hopeful that this will be a source of satisfaction to Americans and a contribution to world peace."

Congress gave permanent status and funds to the Peace Corps on September 22, 1961. Never before, they later agreed, had so little bought so much. Working in forty-six countries overseas, the Peace Corps brightened the American image in the world. In all too many nations the United States had become a symbol of military aggressiveness; of "arrogant power," as Senator Fulbright declared; of support for unpopular, dictatorial governments hated by their own people.

The Peace Corps did much to give the poor of the world a new image of Americans, and to make them want to follow the American rather than Communist way to a better life. In 1965, when American troops were ordered into the Dominican Republic, the Dominican people were furious at the intervention. The cry of "Yankee Go Home!" was raised on every side. But during the worst of the disorders, one group of Americans continued to be completely respected and trusted by the Dominican people—the Peace Corpsmen who had been working on the island.

In December, 1963, less than a month after President Kennedy's assassination, Congress passed a $1,200 million college construction program bill. The following year, disturbed by studies showing that the unemployment rate for high school dropouts was 32 per cent, Congress passed the Economic Opportunity Act of 1964, known as the Anti-Poverty Act.

The act provided for rural conservation camps and urban training centers to give job training to drop-outs. Work-training part-time jobs were provided for 200,000 high school youths to help them stay in school. Part-time jobs were also found for 140,000 college students to keep them on campus. Other grants were made in the act to fight poverty and illiteracy in both urban and rural communities.

Explaining the act as one of the most important in his Great Society program, President Johnson declared, "We want to offer the forgotten fifth of our people opportunity, not doles." In 1965 Congress passed a bill to provide four-year federal scholarships for needy students, about 140,000 each year.

If there was widespread enthusiasm among the youth of America for what the Congress had done for them as scholars, there was little for another piece of legislation that greatly affected them as soldiers—the Selective Service Act.

During 1965–1966 there were widespread protests, in parades and demonstrations, against the unpopular Vietnam War. Some youths burned their draft cards and were arrested for it. Most protesters asked for a change in the act to allow them to serve their country in the Peace Corps instead.

Conscience, they insisted, did not allow them to participate in an undeclared war that millions of students, teachers, ministers, and members of the Senate Foreign Relations Committee felt was morally wrong.

Others demanded that Congress pass a law lowering the voting age to eighteen. "Any country which considers eighteen old enough to die for it," explained one youth, "owes eighteen-year-olds the right to a legal voice in the country's affairs."

Commented Senator J. William Fulbright on the youth protest movement: "In a democracy, dissent is an act of faith. . . . Criticism . . . is an act of patriotism. Today's protesters against the Vietnam War are in good historical company. . . . It is an expression of national conscience and a manifestation of traditional American idealism."

14

Laws on Slavery and Civil Rights

It was a hot August night in 1965, and the Negro people living in the Watts slum area of Los Angeles were in an ugly mood. The government was pouring $2 billion and more annually into California's aerospace industries, creating prosperity among white workers of southern California. But the Negroes—under-educated, discriminated against in employment, herded into a ghetto and harassed by police—were excluded from the comforts and affluence of the white Angelenos.

State police sought to arrest a Negro youth in Watts on a charge of drunken driving. An angry crowd of Negroes quickly gathered to protest the arrest. The incident turned into a flash riot, touching off the powder keg of discontent that underlay all of Watts. Thousands of furious Negroes stormed through the streets, venting their rage and frustration by setting fire to stores and buildings, smashing and burning cars, looting, assaulting and shooting at whites.

"Burn whitey!" was the cry. "Burn whitey, man!"

Fifteen thousand National Guard troops were rushed into southside Los Angeles. The street mobs broke up into guerilla bands, fighting police and troops with guns, bricks, and home-made fire bombs. The battle raged for five terrible days, costing the lives of seven whites and twenty-nine Negroes. More than nine hundred persons were injured, four thousand and more arrested—most of them Negroes.

Property damage was estimated at $200 million. When the riot finally subsided under the pressure of rifles, bayonets, police clubs, tear gas and fire hoses, the community of Watts resembled nothing so much as a battlefield ruin. It had been the most devastating riot in American history.

Former President Eisenhower said sadly that the trouble at Watts showed the nation "becoming atmosphered, you might say, in a policy of lawlessness." Senator Robert Kennedy said that Watts had occurred because the Negro had been made to feel that "the law has been his enemy." Evangelist Billy Graham called Watts "a dress rehearsal for what is to come." President Johnson pleaded, "We must not let anger drown understanding."

One of the young rioters explained to a reporter his notion of why the Negro uprising in Watts had occurred: "You got people who are angry, Jack—you got people who are *extremely* angry!" The roots of that extreme anger went deep, stretching back to the earliest treatment of Negroes brought to America as unwilling slaves from Africa.

Although the first shipload of slaves arrived in the Virginia colony in 1619, the South relied on poor white labor for another century. The slave trade didn't really boom until the eighteenth century. Then, by 1760, there were almost half a million Negro slaves working on Southern plantations.

Following the American Revolution, the nation's leaders were deeply disturbed at the paradox of being a country of "free men"—except for those with black skins. In 1786, Washington wrote Lafayette that he hoped for a plan to abolish slavery "by slow, sure and imperceptible degrees." In his will he emancipated all his own slaves.

Fellow Southerner Thomas Jefferson was equally distressed about the denial to Negroes of the freedom he himself had eloquently advocated for Americans in the Declaration of Independence—"all men are created equal and equally entitled to life, liberty, and the pursuit of happiness."

When a slave insurrection broke out in Virginia in 1800, he wrote, "We are truly to be pitied. I tremble for my country when I reflect that God is just." At Jefferson's insistence, Congress passed an Act to Prohibit the Importation of Slaves in 1807. This law, however, did not stop the illegal slave traffic, which continued to flourish until the Civil War.

By 1819 there was an even balance between the states that barred slavery, in the North, and those that depended upon slaves, in the South. But then Missouri, which had been part of the Louisiana Purchase, applied for admission to the Union as a slave state. North and South were plunged into a struggle for the controlling power in Congress.

The fight ended temporarily with the Missouri Compromise of 1820, worked out by Henry Clay. Missouri was admitted as a slave state, balanced by Maine's admission as a free state. Slavery, moreover, was barred from the Louisiana Purchase territory north of Missouri's southern border, except Missouri.

As the friction between North and South over slavery grew more intense, a Northern abolitionist movement developed, bent on liberating slaves in the South. Plantation owners grew fearful that this agitation might cause their slaves to revolt. They thought this had happened in 1831 when a Virginia slave named Nat Turner, inspired by religious visions, led seventy slaves in a local uprising that killed fifty-seven white persons.

Alarmed that a full-scale Negro revolution was in progress, the South rushed detachments of militia, reinforced by three companies of artillery and detachments from two warships, to put down the "revolution." About a hundred Negroes were massacred; twenty more were arrested, tried, and hanged.

Nat Turner was interviewed in chains before his execution. Asked if the fate he faced had not made him realize his mistake, he replied calmly, "Was not Christ crucified?" And he related the vision that had led him to revolt.

"I saw white spirits and black spirits engaged in battle," he said, "and the sun was darkened. The thunder rolled in the heavens, and blood flowed in streams." It could have been a prophecy of the Civil War. Or of Watts.

Some Southerners discreetly became more humane to their slaves. But some became convinced that only stern and fear-inspiring treatment could prevent additional Nat Turners. In one case that reached the high court of North Carolina, *State v. Mann,* the court ruled grimly, "The power of the master must be absolute, to render the submission of the slave perfect."

Northern abolitionists flooded Congress with antislavery petitions during the 1830's, angering Southern members of both Houses. In 1836 Southern representatives succeeded in putting through a "gag resolution," tabling such petitions automatically so that they could not be heard. Former President John Quincy Adams, who had become a representative, was shouted down when he tried to obtain a hearing for a petition to protect the lives of Northern abolitionists going to the South.

Adams, too, was a prophet. "It's in slavery," he told Alexis de Tocqueville, the French observer of American life, "that are to be found almost all the embarrassments of the present, and the fears of the future."

The westward expansion of America revived the struggle between North and South over the political balance of slave and free states. Once again Henry Clay came to the rescue with the Compromise of 1850, which admitted California as a free state; abolished the slave trade, but not slavery, from the District of Columbia; promised a law to curb runaway slaves; admitted New Mexico and Utah as territories with self-determination.

Congress followed this by passing the Fugitive Slave Act of 1850, providing strong federal aid in apprehending runaway slaves, returning them to their masters, and punishing by fines and imprisonment any who hindered the legal process. This act infuriated abolitionists. Mass meetings were held all over the North to announce publicly the intention to disobey the law. State legislatures in the North passed laws forbidding the use of their jails for detaining runaway slaves.

The drums of civil war grew louder.

On June 2, 1854, Anthony Burns, a runaway Negro slave from Virginia, was ordered to leave the free soil of Massachusetts and return to his master. Thousands of abolitionists met in pro-test meetings. The stores in Boston closed; streets were draped in mourning; a huge coffin was suspended across State Street. A crowd of abolitionists, led by Wendell Phillips and Theodore Parker, tried to snatch Burns from his prison cell.

The frightened mayor of Boston called for federal troops. It took a thousand soldiers and police, with guns leveled, to escort Anthony Burns through the crowds that wanted to rescue him.

"Shame!" yelled the indignant Bostonians. "Kidnapers!" It cost the United States $100,000 to apprehend, detain, and return one runaway slave to his Virginia master.

More fuel to the flames of Northern indignation was added by Harriet Beeeher Stowed's novel, *Uncle Tom's Cabin,* in which Simon Legree came to personify a villainous South. When Lincoln met Mrs. Stowe, he mused aloud, "So you're the little woman who wrote the book that started this great war!"

Both Missouri Compromises were undone in 1854 when Congress passed the Kansas-Nebraska Act, giving settlers of these Louisiana Purchase territories the right to determine for themselves whether they should be slave or free. This law turned

Kansas into a battleground for North and South, both of which rushed squatters into the territory to sway the vote. The nation was soon appalled at the spectacle of "bleeding Kansas," with Northern and Southern sympathizers fighting each other in a preview of the major conflict to come.

But the proslavery forces won their most decisive victory in the Supreme Court, rather than in Congress or the territories. In 1846 Dr. John Emerson of Missouri took his slave, Dred Scott, to Illinois and the Wisconsin territory, both of them free soil. Upon returning to Missouri, Dred Scott sued in the state courts for his freedom, claiming he had become free through his residence on free soil. The case eventually reached the Supreme Court, which ruled against him in 1858.

Chief Justice Roger B. Taney declared that no Negro slave or descendant could be a U.S. citizen, and therefore had no right to sue in federal courts. He also stated that Congress had no right to prohibit slavery in the territories, and that the Missouri Compromise had been unconstitutional, because it deprived Southerners of their slave property without due process of law. The South was delighted by the Dred Scott decision.

The North was furious. "The Court has abdicated its just functions and descended into the political arena," accused Horace Greeley in the influential New York *Tribune.* "It has sullied its ermine; it has draggled and polluted its garments in the filth of pro-slavery politics."

In 1858 Lincoln warned, "A house divided against itself cannot stand. I believe this government cannot endure permanently half slave and half free. . . . It will become all one thing, or all the other."

South Carolina made Lincoln's election in 1860 the occasion for an ordinance of secession, which brought on the Civil War. In fighting this war, Lincoln made it clear that his purpose was not to abolish slavery but to preserve the Union. It was largely the pressure of Horace Greeley, however, that forced his hand and made him issue the Emancipation Proclamation, on January 1, 1863, even though Lincoln feared that this might alienate Northern conservatives and solidify Southern resistance.

In December, 1865, the abolition of slavery became the Thirteenth Amendment to the Constitution. At long last the Negro was recognized as a full American citizen under the law. But it was another matter to translate that law into reality.

Following the Civil War, and the succession of Andrew Johnson to the Presidency after the assassination of Lincoln, the Northern desire for revenge prevailed. It was augmented by many Northern opportunists who saw the chance to win crooked fortunes through manipulating Negroes raised to positions of authority in the new South.

In 1865, Congress passed the Freedmen's Bureau Act, establishing that agency in the War Department to protect the rights of freed slaves and supervise the disposition of "abandoned lands" in the South, for the benefit of Negroes.

The following year Congress passed the Civil Rights Bill of 1866, over Johnson's veto, conferring citizenship upon the Negro and guaranteeing him equality of treatment before the law. Outraged Southern states retaliated by passing the Black Codes, restricting Negroes' economic and political activities.

In angry reply, Congress proposed the Fourteenth Amendment to the Constitution, guaranteeing full citizenship to all persons born or naturalized in the United States; preventing any state from passing a law to deprive such person of life, liberty or property without due process of law and guaranteeing him the "equal protection of the laws." This amendment was ratified and admitted to the Constitution in 1868.

The Southerners fought the Reconstruction period in every way they could. Secret societies like the Ku Klux Klan were used to terrify Negroes into renouncing their political power.

Negroes were denied jobs and forced to continue using segregated facilities. Southern evasion of the Fourteenth and Fifteenth Amendments was so flagrant that Congress was forced to pass the Enforcement Acts of 1870 and 1871 imposing heavy penalties for violations of the amendments.

But by 1869 conservative whites in the Southern states had regained control. Radical Republicans of the North, far less interested in the Negro than in their own political advantage, withdrew federal troops completely by 1877.

In 1875 Congress went through the motions of slapping Southern wrists by passing a Civil Rights Act prohibiting discrimination in public acts. The Supreme Court nullified this the following year, in *United States v. Cruikshank,* calling it unconstitutional because it failed to forbid discriminatory acts by individuals as well as by states.

Another blow to civil rights fell in 1883, when the Supreme Court, ruling in *United States v. Harris,* asserted that neither the Fourteenth nor Fifteenth Amendment was designed to take from the states their control over elections. The South quickly deprived Negroes of their voting rights through imposing poll taxes, literacy tests, and white-only primary elections.

Negro hopes were dealt another severe setback in 1896, when the Supreme Court, in *Plessy v. Ferguson,* ruled that Louisiana was not violating the Fourteenth Amendment by a law requiring railroads to segregate Negroes, if equal accommodations were provided for both races. This "separate but equal" principle became the defense of the South in racially segregating its schools, restaurants, transportation, and public facilities.

All through the first part of the twentieth century, Negroes remained segregated in the South, discriminated against in the North, subjected to terror by such vigilante groups as the Ku Klux Klan. When a seventeen-year-old Negro boy accidentally swam over the boundary of a "white" beach on Lake Michigan, it caused the terrible Chicago race riot of 1919. Negroes and white progressives all over America became incensed when nine Negro youths were convicted in an Alabama court of a serious felony on trumped-up charges—the celebrated Scottsboro case in 1931.

More and more the American Negro felt helpless, frustrated, and bitter over every betrayal of the Emancipation Proclamation, decade after decade, denying him the equal rights he had been promised as an American citizen.

When the Supreme Court changed, during the Roosevelt administration, from the conservative "nine old men" who had killed the NRA to a younger and more liberal body, a new attitude toward the rights of the Negro began to appear. The first sign was in 1938, when a Negro appealed to the Supreme Court to compel the State of Missouri to order his admission into the University of Missouri law school.

The Court did not then upset the "separate but equal" ruling. It did, however, state that since Missouri had no separate and equal law school for Negroes, it was obliged to admit the Negro applicant to the University of Missouri law school.

Negroes began to hope that justice was possible when the Supreme Court, in 1940, reversed a Florida court's death sentence against a group of Negro tenant farmers who had been tortured into a confession (*Chambers v. Florida*).

"Under our constitutional system," said Justice Hugo Black for the majority finding a violation of the Fourteenth Amendment, "courts stand against any winds that blow as havens of refuge for those who might otherwise suffer because they are nonconforming victims of prejudice and public excitement."

Clearly, America was beginning to find its conscience.

In 1941 President Roosevelt, using his wartime emergency powers, ordered all federal agencies to refuse government war production contracts to any firms which practiced discrimination in employment. This was the beginning of Fair Employment Practice codes subsequently adopted by many states.

The Democratic administrations of both Roosevelt and Truman, however, were unable to get Congress to pass new-civil rights acts. Although the Democrats controlled Congress, many were Southerners unalterably opposed to civil rights. They threatened to filibuster—and did—to keep any civil rights legislation from coming to a vote.

The Supreme Court, meanwhile, continued tearing down legal fences separating the races. In 1950 they declared in two cases *Sweatt v. Painter* and *McLaurin v. Oklahoma*—that segregated graduate schools could not really be equal with white institutions, and so were in violation of the "equal protection" clause of the Fourteenth Amendment.

But the really earth-shaking Supreme Court decision came in 1954, in the case of *Brown v. Board of Education of Topeka*. For the first time the Court was ruling not just on admission to universities for a few brilliant Negroes, but on the question of segregation in the whole public school system.

"In these days," declared Chief Justice Earl Warren, "it is doubtful that any child may reasonably be expected to succeed in life if he is denied the opportunity of an education. Such an opportunity, where the state has undertaken to provide it, is a right which must be made available to all on equal terms." By a unanimous decision, the Supreme Court reversed the "separate but equal" concept, and ruled that segregation of public schools by race was unconstitutional.

The decision galvanized the civil rights movement in America. Negro organizations and civil rights groups like the NAACP, CORE, SNCC, the Southern Christian Leadership Conference, the Urban League, the Negro Labor Council, and the Black Muslims began to press feverishly for Negro rights as guaranteed by the Constitution and Supreme Court rulings.

In September, 1957, nine Negro students attempted to enroll in Central High School at Little Rock, Arkansas. Under orders from Governor Orval Faubus, the state's National Guard barred their entrance—a clear violation of the Supreme Court's decree. Angrily President Eisenhower issued a proclamation to "command all persons engaged in such obstruction of justice to cease and desist therefrom and to disperse forthwith.

"The Federal law . . . cannot be flouted with impunity by any individual or any mob of extremists," he declared. "I will use the full power of the United States, including whatever force may be necessary, to prevent any obstruction of the law and to carry out the orders of the Federal Court." Federal troops were ordered to Little Rock to quell disorders and protect the rights of the Negro students to register and attend.

With the other two branches of government—the Judiciary and Executive—acting to secure the Negro's civil rights, Congress finally passed legislation. The Civil Rights Act of 1957, passed over strong Southern opposition, established a civil rights division in the Department of Justice to stop violation of Negro voting rights. But the act also repealed a Reconstruction statute that allowed the President to use federal troops to enforce civil rights law.

One provision of the act set up a Civil Rights Commission to study violations of civil rights. As a result of this report, Congress passed the Civil Rights Act of 1960, but only after two months of Senate debate and a nine-day filibuster. The act established fines and prison terms for anyone using threats or force in defiance of a federal court order to prevent Negroes from voting.

Now Negro leaders began to take steps themselves to translate American laws into American realities. There were sit-in demonstrations, "freedom rides" to the South, protest marches, voting registration campaigns, bus and store boycotts, Negro attempts to register in all-white schools. Joining in this crusade were many white sympathizers and clergy, who sang the spiritual anthem of the civil rights movement, "We Shall Overcome." Its leader, in the eye of the storm, was Rev. Martin Luther King of the Southern Christian Leadership Conference, who followed Gandhi's example of nonviolent civil disobedience.

Fighting back, conservative whites in the South organized White Citizens Councils to thward the Negro thrust for legal and social equality. The Ku Klux Klan began wearing hoods and burning crosses again. When Klansmen were arrested for the murders of civil rights workers, Southern juries promptly acquitted them. Many Negro homes and churches in the South were bombed by fanatical segregationists.

Nothing outraged the American people, and won powerful sympathy for the Negro cause, like TV newsreel pictures of Birmingham, Alabama, Safety Commissioner Eugene (Bull) Connor and his police dispersing a Negro demonstration with high-pressure fire hoses and vicious police dogs, while many of the peaceful demonstrators were praying. These films sickened many moderate Southerners, too, and new voices began to be raised in the South against persecution of the Negro.

In June, 1963, Governor George Wallace of Alabama sought to prevent two Negro students from entering the University of Alabama by "standing in the schoolhouse door." President John Kennedy angrily federalized the state's National Guard and sternly ordered Wallace not to interfere with the desegregation of the university. Wallace gave in.

"When Americans are sent to Vietnam or West Berlin we do not ask for whites only," Kennedy declared. "It ought to be possible, therefore, for American students of any color to attend any public institution they select without having to be backed up by troops. . . . One hundred years of delay have passed since President Lincoln freed the slaves, yet their heirs, their grandsons, are not fully free."

In August, Martin Luther King dramatized American injustice against the Negro by a great march of 200,000 persons, Negro and white, on Washington, D.C. The marchers demanded "Freedom—Now." In an eloquent speech, "I Have a Dream," King looked forward to the day when a new, fully democratic America would practice as well as preach equality, justice, brotherhood.

The following year Congress passed the Civil Rights Act of 1964, after invoking cloture to end a Southern filibuster. Discrimination was forbidden in hotels, restaurants, theaters, and other public places. The Attorney General was authorized to file suits for any persons discriminated against. Discrimination was forbidden by either employers or labor unions. Federal funds were denied to any project in which discrimination was found. The Act also forbade the use of different requirements for Negroes and whites in voting registration.

In January, 1964, a bill passed two years earlier by Congress became the Twenty-fourth Amendment to the Constitution, stipulating that the right to vote in federal elections cannot be denied for failure to pay a poll tax or any other tax, thus ending one important technique by which the South had for a century been able to keep Negroes from voting.

Angered by the slaying of a woman civil rights worker in March, 1965, President Johnson grimly declared war on the Ku Klux Klan as a "hooded society of bigots." The House Un-American Activities Committee, headed by a Louisiana Democrat, conducted an investigation into Klan activities. Some Klan leaders were indicted. The Klan's ability to enforce Southern white supremacy by terror was clearly at an end, although Southern juries are reluctant to convict Klan defendants.

In August Congress passed the 1965 Voting Rights Act authorizing federal examiners to be sent into any state where discriminatory voting practices persisted, to register Negro voters and guarantee their right to the ballot.

The significance of the new civil rights legislation of the 1960's became evident in the spring of 1966. For the first time in Alabama history, not a single candidate for governor uttered a word in defense of white supremacy. Alabama now had hundreds of thousands of registered Negro voters. Many candidates eagerly shook their hands and sought their votes.

It began to look like a bright new day for the South. But in the same month that Congress passed the 1965 Voting Rights Act, the terrible riots in Watts occurred, followed by rioting in other cities as well.

Militant young Negro leaders raised the cry of "Black Power!" demanding full civil rights immediately. They proposed to implement their rallying cry of "Black Power" by a show of strength at the polls, and more aggressive tactics. They objected to a continuation of Martin Luther King's policies of non-violence and peaceful demonstrations that included white liberals.

The riots and cries of "Black Power!" frightened many white Americans, who began to feel that the Negro movement was proceeding at too fast a pace. This reaction, called the "white backlash" brought segregationist candidates into the open, who ran for office on an anti-civil rights platform. The pressure on Congress made itself felt in the defeat of the 1966 Civil Rights Act—the first setback for the Johnson administration on civil rights legislation.

In the meantime, moderate, responsible Negroes led by Roy Wilkins (NAACP) repudiated the phrase "Black Power," insisting that they needed and wanted the support of white Americans.

The new laws are rapidly changing life in America for the Negro people. But the change can never be rapid enough for the millions who are trapped in ghetto slums, deprived of a good education, decent job opportunities, and their fair share of the

Great Society. While the frightening specter of "Black Power" may slow Negro progress, it is likely to be only a temporary setback. White Americans are realizing more and more that Negroes are Americans, too; and that these fellow Americans must be drawn into the mainstream of American life if we are to have genuine democracy.

15

Your Laws—Yesterday, Today and Tomorrow

The laws that have changed our nation have taken us a long way from the America of 1776. Yet although our lawmakers have sought to keep pace with the changing world, and our place in it, they have remained faithful to our first and basic laws—the American Constitution and the Bill of Rights.

It seems astonishing that the original Founders of our code of law could have been so wise and far-sighted in establishing such durable concepts of freedom, of order, and of justice. The explanation is that these laws did not spring magically out of the heads of the Founding Fathers.

They were derived from Western legal systems of the eleventh and twelfth centuries. These, in turn, were derived from Roman law, Greek philosophy, Hebrew and Christian ethics.

"The law of every country of Europe," explained English statesman Edmund Burke two hundred years ago, "is derived from the same sources." It was this concept of law that the first settlers of America brought with them from England, to become the foundation of American law. Thus, essentially, the Constitution and the Bill of Rights represent the distillation of the finest legal wisdom man has been capable of in the last twenty centuries of human experience.

America has thrived and grown on the shoulders of those basic laws, adding to and modifying them as the needs of the people required. War hysteria, unhappily, has sometimes made Americans forget the precious safeguards of our Bill of Rights.

But thanks principally to the Civil Liberties Union, and in later years the Supreme Court, the rights of Americans under the Bill of Rights have been stoutly defended and protected. Americans can never afford to forget that their own nation was founded in revolution, in protest, in speaking out against injustice. When the day comes that *any* American can be silenced, then *no* American's freedom of speech is safe.

This is why the Bill of Rights was made a vital part of the American Constitution. It is our most powerful bulwark against dictatorship. It is our guarantee that we will continue to be a nation governed by law, not by individuals—whose ideas of right and wrong can change with each individual.

Our most serious legislative problem in the future stems from the steadily expanding population explosion. The larger our population grows, the more difficult it becomes for the voice of individual citizens to be heard by their representatives in Congress. Too often the lobbies of special interests in Washington speak louder than the voice of the people.

But Americans today are making their will known largely by their choice of the presidential candidate and his party. Acting on this mandate from the people, the President generally proposes the legislative program that is subsequently enacted by the Congress.

Laws that change America will continue to change her in the future as the nation advances into the Space Age. We can expect to see bold new laws defining the rights of Americans as space travelers, as homesteaders on other planets, as entrepreneurs in space projects. And it is almost certain that there will be laws regulating oceanographic development.

But what, it is to be hoped, will *not* change is the foundation of such new laws in the Constitution and Bill of Rights.

Only in this way can Americans be guaranteed the exciting blessings of the future, along with the protection of their heritage of freedom and democracy from the past.

BIBLIOGRAPHY

Allen, Frederick Lewis. *Only Yesterday.* New York: Bantam Books, 1946.

Archer, Jules. *Fighting Journalist: Horace Greeley.* New York: Julian Messner, Inc., 1966.

Barck, Oscar T., Jr. *A History of the United States Since 1945.* New York: Dell Publishing Co., Inc., 1965.

Baruch, Bernard M. *The Public Years.* New York: Holt, Rinehart and Winston, 1960.

Berman, Harold J. (ed.). *Talks on American Law.* New York: Vintage Books, 1961.

Constitution of Our United States. Chicago: Rand McNally & Co., 1936.

Day Donald (ed.). *Woodrow Wilson's Own Story.* Boston: Little, Brown and Company, 1952.

Eisenhower, Dwight D. *Mandate for Change.* New York: Doubleday & Company, Inc., 1963.

——. *Waging Peace.* New York: Doubleday & Company, Inc., 1965.

Gunther, John. *Inside U.S.A.* New York and London: Harper & Brothers, 1947.

Hassett, William D. *Off the Record with FDR.* London: George Allen & Unwin Ltd., 1960.

Heffner, Richard D. *A Documentary History of the United States.* New York: New American Library, 1952.

Holbrook, Stewart H. *Dreamers of the American Dream.* New York: Doubleday & Company, Inc., 1957.

Hutchins, Robert M. *Two Faces of Federalism.* Santa Barbara, California: Center for the Study of Democratic Institutions, 1961.

Kull, Irving S. and Nell M. *An Encyclopedia of American History.* New York: Popular Library, Inc., 1965.

Markmann, Charles' Lam. *The Noblest Cry.* New York: St. Martin Press, 1965.

Miers, Earl Schenck (ed.). *The American Story.* London: George Allen and Unwin, Ltd., 1957.

Myers, Gustavus. *History of the Great American Fortunes.* New York: The Modern Library, Inc.

Neustadt, Richard E. *Presidential Power.* New York: John Wiley & Sons, Inc., 1960.

Nevins, Allan, and Henry Steel Commager. *A Pocket History of the United States.* New York: Washington Square Press, Inc., 1942.

Padoyer, Saul K. *The Living U.S. Constitution.* New York: New American Library, 1953.

Peltason, Jack W., and James M. Burns. *Functions and Policies of American Government.* Englewood Cliffs, N.J.: Prentice-Hall, Inc., 1958.

Pierson, George Wilson. *Tocqueville in America.* New York: Doubleday & Company, Inc., 1959.

Rollins, Alfred B. Jr. *Woodrow Wilson and the New America.* New York: Dell Publishing Co., Inc.

Seldes, George. *One Thousand Americans.* New York: Boni & Gaer, 1947.

Snyder, Louis L. (ed.). *They Saw It Happen.* Harrisburg, Pa.: The Stackpole Company, 1951.

Stimpson, George. *A Book About American History.* New York: Harper & Brothers, 1956.

Syrett, Harold C. (ed.). *American Historical Documents.* New York: Barnes & Noble, Inc., 1960.

Thornton, Willis. *Fable, Fact and History.* Philadelphia: Chilton Books, 1957.

Truman, Harry S. *Years of Trial and Hope.* New York: New American Library, 1965.

Woods, John A. *Roosevelt and Modern America.* New York: Collier Books, 1962.

Woodward, William E. *The Way Our People Lived.* New York: Washington Square Press, Inc., 1965.